TRUST AND OBEY

TRUST AND OBEY

Compiled by Eugene Carvalho

Trust and Obey

Copyright © 2020 by Eugene Carvalho

ISBN: 978-1542409285

Printed in the United States of America

To the Body of Christ.
May this compilation bless you richly!
With love…

TABLE OF CONTENTS

PURPOSE AND ACKNOWLEDGEMENTS

The infallible Word of God for faith and conduct informs us that the Holy Spirit gives gifts to men and women of the Body of Christ. It states: "the gifts edify the body for the building up of the saints" (Eph. 4:12). I hope the talents and gifts the Lord has given me will be a blessing to someone else through the reading of this compilation.

I am grateful for the love from all family members, especially my wife Mercedes. I am also grateful for the knowledge, wisdom and love of many pastors, teachers, and saints that the Lord has used to bless me.

Chapter One

TRUST AND OBEY

When we examine the integrity of Daniel we see he would not bow down to the ungodly laws of the king, but instead trusted and obeyed God. The Bible informs us, 'Then the king gave orders, and Daniel was brought in and cast into the lions' den. The king spoke and said to Daniel, 'Your God whom you constantly serve will Himself deliver you.' And a stone was brought and laid over the mouth of the den; and the king sealed it with his own signet ring and with the signet rings of his nobles, so that nothing might be changed in regard to Daniel. Then the king went off to his palace and spent the night fasting, and no entertainment was brought before him; and his sleep fled from him. Then the king arose with the dawn, at the break of day, and went in haste to the lions' den. And when he had come near the den to Daniel, he cried out with a troubled voice. The king spoke and said to Daniel, 'Daniel, servant of the living God, has your God, whom you constantly serve, been able to deliver you from the lions?' Then Daniel spoke to the king, 'O king, live forever! My God sent His angel and shut the lions' mouths, and they have not harmed me, inasmuch as I was found innocent before Him; and also toward you, O king, I have committed no crime.' Then the king was very pleased and gave orders for Daniel to be taken up out of the den. So Daniel was taken up out of the den, and no injury whatever was found on him, because he had trusted in his God" (Da. 6:16-23).[1]

Being led by the Holy Spirit, and trusting and obeying God, is vital in these last days. The Bible says, "We are destroying speculations and every lofty thing raised up against the knowledge of God, and we are taking every thought captive to the obedience of Christ, and we are ready to punish all disobedience, whenever your obedience is complete" (2 Cor. 10:5-6).

Let's examine a few scriptures concerning obedience. (1) "Being found in appearance as a man, He humbled Himself by becoming obedient to the point of death, even death on a cross" (Phil. 2:8). (2) "For as through the one man's disobedience the many were made sinners, even so through the obedience of the One the many will be made righteous" (Ro. 5:19). And lastly, "Submit therefore to God. Resist the devil and he will flee from you. Draw near to God and He will draw near to you. Cleanse your hands, you sinners; and purify your hearts, you double-minded. Be miserable and mourn and weep; let your laughter be turned into mourning and your joy to gloom. Humble yourselves in the presence of the Lord, and He will exalt you" (Jas. 4:7-10).

Therefore, let's examine the Old and New Testament scriptures that discuss trust and obey. They will give you fresh revelation, build you faith, renew your mind, and be a blessing to you.

---

[1] From this point forward all Scripture quotations, unless otherwise noted, are from the *New American Standard Bible*.

TRUST IN THE OLD TESTAMENT

IN THE BOOK OF EXODUS

Breach of Trust

"If a man gives his neighbor money or goods to keep for him and it is stolen from the man's house, if the thief is caught, he shall pay double. If the thief is not caught, then the owner of the house shall appear before the judges, to determine whether he laid his hands on his neighbor's property. For every breach of trust, whether it is for ox, for donkey, for sheep, for clothing, or for any lost thing about which one says, 'This is it,' the case of both parties shall come before the judges; he whom the judges condemn shall pay double to his neighbor" (Ex. 22:7-9).

IN THE BOOK OF DEUTEROMONY

You Did Not Trust the Lord your God

"Yet you were not willing to go up, but rebelled against the command of the Lord your God; and you grumbled in your tents and said, 'Because the Lord hates us, He has brought us out of the land of Egypt to deliver us into the hand of the Amorites to destroy us. Where can we go up? Our brethren have made our hearts melt, saying, 'The people are bigger and taller than we; the cities are large and fortified to heaven. And

besides, we saw the sons of the Anakim there.'"
Then I said to you, 'Do not be shocked, nor fear
them. The Lord your God who goes before you
will Himself fight on your behalf, just as He did
for you in Egypt before your eyes, and in the
wilderness where you saw how the Lord your
God carried you, just as a man carries his son, in
all the way which you have walked until you
came to this place.' But for all this, you did not
trust the Lord your God, who goes before you on
your way, to seek out a place for you to encamp,
in fire by night and cloud by day, to show you the
way in which you should go" (Dt. 1:26-33).

IN THE BOOK OF JUDGES

The Men of Shechem Put their Trust in Him

"Now Gaal the son of Ebed came with his
relatives, and crossed over into Shechem; and the
men of Shechem put their trust in him. They went
out into the field and gathered the grapes of their
vineyards and trod them, and held a festival; and
they went into the house of their god, and ate and
drank and cursed Abimelech. Then Gaal the son of
Ebed said, 'Who is Abimelech, and who is
Shechem, that we should serve him? Is he not the
son of Jerubbaal, and is Zebul not his lieutenant?
Serve the men of Hamor the father of Shechem;
but why should we serve him? Would, therefore,
that this people were under my authority! Then I
would remove Abimelech.' And he said to

Abimelech, 'Increase your army and come out'"
(Jdg. 9:26-29).

But Sihon Did Not Trust Israel

"Now Jephthah sent messengers to the king
of the sons of Ammon, saying, 'What is between
you and me, that you have come to me to fight
against my land?' The king of the sons of Ammon
said to the messengers of Jephthah, 'Because Israel
took away my land when they came up from
Egypt, from the Arnon as far as the Jabbok and the
Jordan; therefore, return them peaceably now.' But
Jephthah sent messengers again to the king of the
sons of Ammon, and they said to him, 'Thus says
Jephthah, 'Israel did not take away the land of
Moab nor the land of the sons of Ammon. For
when they came up from Egypt, and Israel went
through the wilderness to the Red Sea and came to
Kadesh, then Israel sent messengers to the king of
Edom, saying, 'Please let us pass through your
land,' but the king of Edom would not listen. And
they also sent to the king of Moab, but he would
not consent. So Israel remained at Kadesh. Then
they went through the wilderness and around the
land of Edom and the land of Moab, and came to
the east side of the land of Moab, and they camped
beyond the Arnon; but they did not enter the
territory of Moab, for the Arnon was the border of
Moab. And Israel sent messengers to Sihon king of
the Amorites, the king of Heshbon, and Israel said
to him, 'Please let us pass through your land to

our place.' But Sihon did not trust Israel to pass through his territory; so Sihon gathered all his people and camped in Jahaz and fought with Israel. The Lord, the God of Israel, gave Sihon and all his people into the hand of Israel, and they defeated them; so Israel possessed all the land of the Amorites, the inhabitants of that country. So they possessed all the territory of the Amorites, from the Arnon as far as the Jabbok, and from the wilderness as far as the Jordan. Since now the Lord, the God of Israel, drove out the Amorites from before His people Israel, are you then to possess it? Do you not possess what Chemosh your god gives you to possess? So whatever the Lord our God has driven out before us, we will possess it. Now are you any better than Balak the son of Zippor, king of Moab? Did he ever strive with Israel, or did he ever fight against them? While Israel lived in Heshbon and its villages, and in Aroer and its villages, and in all the cities that are on the banks of the Arnon, three hundred years, why did you not recover them within that time? I therefore have not sinned against you, but you are doing me wrong by making war against me; may the Lord, the Judge, judge today between the sons of Israel and the sons of Ammon.'" But the king of the sons of Ammon disregarded the message which Jephthah sent him" (Jdg. 11:12-28).

Chapter Two

IN THE BOOK OF 2 KINGS

We Trust in the Lord Our God

"Then Rabshakeh said to them, "Say now to Hezekiah, 'Thus says the great king, the king of Assyria, 'What is this confidence that you have? You say (but they are only empty words), 'I have counsel and strength for the war.' Now on whom do you rely, that you have rebelled against me? Now behold, you rely on the staff of this crushed reed, even on Egypt; on which if a man leans, it will go into his hand and pierce it. So is Pharaoh king of Egypt to all who rely on him. But if you say to me, 'We trust in the Lord our God,' is it not He whose high places and whose altars Hezekiah has taken away, and has said to Judah and to Jerusalem, 'You shall worship before this altar in Jerusalem'? Now therefore, come, make a bargain with my master the king of Assyria, and I will give you two thousand horses, if you are able on your part to set riders on them. How then can you repulse one official of the least of my master's servants, and rely on Egypt for chariots and for horsemen? Have I now come up without the Lord's approval against this place to destroy it? The Lord said to me, 'Go up against this land and destroy it'" (2Ki. 18:19-25).

Chapter Two

Nor Let Hezekiah Make You Trust in the Lord

"Then Rabshakeh stood and cried with a loud voice in Judean, saying, 'Hear the word of the great king, the king of Assyria. Thus says the king, 'Do not let Hezekiah deceive you, for he will not be able to deliver you from my hand; nor let Hezekiah make you trust in the Lord, saying, "The Lord will surely deliver us, and this city will not be given into the hand of the king of Assyria.' Do not listen to Hezekiah, for thus says the king of Assyria, 'Make your peace with me and come out to me, and eat each of his vine and each of his fig tree and drink each of the waters of his own cistern, until I come and take you away to a land like your own land, a land of grain and new wine, a land of bread and vineyards, a land of olive trees and honey, that you may live and not die.' But do not listen to Hezekiah when he misleads you, saying, 'The Lord will deliver us.' Has any one of the gods of the nations delivered his land from the hand of the king of Assyria? Where are the gods of Hamath and Arpad? Where are the gods of Sepharvaim, Hena and Ivvah? Have they delivered Samaria from my hand? Who among all the gods of the lands have delivered their land from my hand, that the Lord should deliver Jerusalem from my hand'" (2Ki. 18:28-35)?

Chapter Two

In Who You Trust Deceive You

"Then Rabshakeh returned and found the king of Assyria fighting against Libnah, for he had heard that the king had left Lachish. When he heard them say concerning Tirhakah king of Cush, 'Behold, he has come out to fight against you,' he sent messengers again to Hezekiah saying, 'Thus you shall say to Hezekiah king of Judah, 'Do not let your God in whom you trust deceive you saying, "Jerusalem will not be given into the hand of the king of Assyria.' Behold, you have heard what the kings of Assyria have done to all the lands, destroying them completely. So will you be spared? Did the gods of those nations which my fathers destroyed deliver them, even Gozan and Haran and Rezeph and the sons of Eden who were in Telassar? Where is the king of Hamath, the king of Arpad, the king of the city of Sepharvaim, and of Hena and Ivvah'" (2Ki. 19:8-13)?

IN THE BOOK OF 1 CHRONICLES

Appointed in their Office of Trust

"Now the gatekeepers were Shallum and Akkub and Talmon and Ahiman and their relatives (Shallum the chief being stationed until now at the king's gate to the east). These were the gatekeepers for the camp of the sons of Levi. Shallum the son of Kore, the son of Ebiasaph, the son of Korah, and his relatives of his father's house, the Korahites, were over the work of the service, keepers of the thresholds of the tent; and their fathers had been over the camp of the Lord, keepers of the entrance. Phinehas the son of Eleazar was ruler over them previously, and the Lord was with him. Zechariah the son of Meshelemiah was gatekeeper of the entrance of the tent of meeting. All these who were chosen to be gatekeepers at the thresholds were 212. These were enrolled by genealogy in their villages, whom David and Samuel the seer appointed in their office of trust. So they and their sons had charge of the gates of the house of the Lord, even the house of the tent, as guards. The gatekeepers were on the four sides, to the east, west, north and south. Their relatives in their villages were to come in every seven days from time to time to be with them; for the four chief gatekeepers who were Levites, were in an office of trust, and were over the chambers and over the treasuries in the house of God. They spent the night around the house of God, because the watch was committed to them; and they were in charge of opening it morning by morning" (1Ch. 9:17-27).

IN THE BOOK OF 2 CHRONICLES

For We Trust in You and In Your Name

"Now Zerah the Ethiopian came out against them with an army of a million men and 300 chariots, and he came to Mareshah. So Asa went out to meet him, and they drew up in battle formation in the valley of Zephathah at Mareshah. Then Asa called to the Lord his God and said, 'Lord, there is no one besides You to help in the battle between the powerful and those who have no strength; so help us, O Lord our God, for we trust in You, and in Your name have come against this multitude. O Lord, You are our God; let not man prevail against You.' So the Lord routed the Ethiopians before Asa and before Judah, and the Ethiopians fled. Asa and the people who were with him pursued them as far as Gerar; and so many Ethiopians fell that they could not recover, for they were shattered before the Lord and before His army. And they carried away very much plunder. They destroyed all the cities around Gerar, for the dread of the Lord had fallen on them; and they despoiled all the cities, for there was much plunder in them. They also struck down those who owned livestock, and they carried away large numbers of sheep and camels. Then they returned to Jerusalem" (2Ch. 14:9-15).

Put Your Trust in the Lord and You We Be Established

"They rose early in the morning and went out to the wilderness of Tekoa; and when they went out, Jehoshaphat stood and said, 'Listen to me, O Judah and inhabitants of Jerusalem, put your trust in the Lord your God and you will be established. Put your trust in His prophets and succeed.' When he had consulted with the people, he appointed those who sang to the Lord and those who praised Him in holy attire, as they went out before the army and said, 'Give thanks to the Lord, for His lovingkindness is everlasting.' When they began singing and praising, the Lord set ambushes against the sons of Ammon, Moab and Mount Seir, who had come against Judah; so they were routed. For the sons of Ammon and Moab rose up against the inhabitants of Mount Seir destroying them completely; and when they had finished with the inhabitants of Seir, they helped to destroy one another" (2Ch. 20:20-23).

IN THE BOOK OF JOB

He Put No Trust Even In His Servants

"Now a word was brought to me stealthily, And my ear received a whisper of it. Amid disquieting thoughts from the visions of the night, When deep sleep falls on men, Dread came upon me, and trembling, And made all my bones shake. Then a spirit passed by my face; The hair of my flesh bristled up. It stood still, but I could not discern its appearance; A form was before my eyes; There was silence, then I heard a voice: Can mankind be just before God? Can a man be pure before his Maker? He puts no trust even in His servants; And against His angels He charges error. How much more those who dwell in houses of clay, Whose foundation is in the dust, Who are crushed before the moth! Between morning and evening they are broken in pieces; Unobserved, they perish forever. Is not their tent-cord plucked up within them? They die, yet without wisdom"' (Job 4:12-21).

Whose Trust a Spider's Web

"Can the papyrus grow up without a marsh? Can the rushes grow without water? While it is still green and not cut down, Yet it withers before any other plant. So are the paths of all who forget God; And the hope of the godless will perish, Whose confidence is fragile, And whose trust a spider's web. He trusts in his house, but it does not stand; He holds fast to it, but it does not endure. He thrives before the sun, And his shoots spread out over his garden. His roots wrap around a rock pile, He grasps a house of stones. If he is removed from his place, Then it will deny him, saying, 'I never saw you.' Behold, this is the joy of His way; And out of the dust others will spring. Lo, God will not reject a man of integrity, Nor will He support the evildoers. He will yet fill your mouth with laughter And your lips with shouting. Those who hate you will be clothed with shame, And the tent of the wicked will be no longer" (Job 8:11-22).

Chapter Two

You Would Trust, Because There is Hope

"If you would direct your heart right And spread out your hand to Him, If iniquity is in your hand, put it far away, And do not let wickedness dwell in your tents; Then, indeed, you could lift up your face without moral defect, And you would be steadfast and not fear. For you would forget your trouble, As waters that have passed by, you would remember it. Your life would be brighter than noonday; Darkness would be like the morning. Then you would trust, because there is hope; And you would look around and rest securely. You would lie down and none would disturb you, And many would entreat your favor. But the eyes of the wicked will fail, And there will be no escape for them; And their hope is to breathe their last" (Job 11:13-20).

He Puts No Trust in His Holy Ones

"Were you the first man to be born, Or were you brought forth before the hills? Do you hear the secret counsel of God, And limit wisdom to yourself? What do you know that we do not know? What do you understand that we do not? Both the gray-haired and the aged are among us, Older than your father. Are the consolations of God too small for you, Even the word spoken gently with you? Why does your heart carry you away? And why do your eyes flash, That you should turn your spirit against God And allow such words to go out of your mouth? What is man, that he should be pure, Or he who is born of a woman, that he should be righteous? Behold, He puts no trust in His holy ones, And the heavens are not pure in His sight; How much less one who is detestable and corrupt, Man, who drinks iniquity like water" (Job 15:7-16)!

Let Him Not Trust in Emptiness

"I will tell you, listen to me; And what I have seen I will also declare; What wise men have told, And have not concealed from their fathers, To whom alone the land was given, And no alien passed among them. The wicked man writhes in pain all his days, And numbered are the years stored up for the ruthless. Sounds of terror are in his ears; While at peace the destroyer comes upon him. He does not believe that he will return from darkness, And he is destined for the sword. He wanders about for food, saying, 'Where is it?' He knows that a day of darkness is at hand. Distress and anguish terrify him, They overpower him like a king ready for the attack, Because he has stretched out his hand against God And conducts himself arrogantly against the Almighty. He rushes headlong at Him With his massive shield. For he has covered his face with his fat And made his thighs heavy with flesh. He has lived in desolate cities, In houses no one would inhabit, Which are destined to become ruins. He will not become rich, nor will his wealth endure; And his grain will not bend down to the ground. He will not escape from darkness; The flame will wither his shoots, And by the breath of His mouth he will go away. Let him not trust in emptiness, deceiving himself; For emptiness will be his reward. It will be accomplished before his time, And his palm branch will not be green. He will drop off his unripe grape like the vine, And will cast off his flower like the olive tree. For the company of the godless is barren, And fire consumes the tents of the corrupt. They conceive mischief and bring forth iniquity, And their mind prepares deception" (Job 15:17-35).

Called Fine Gold My Trust

"If I have put my confidence in gold, And called fine gold my trust, If I have gloated because my wealth was great, And because my hand had secured so much; If I have looked at the sun when it shone Or the moon going in splendor, And my heart became secretly enticed, And my hand threw a kiss from my mouth, That too would have been an iniquity calling for judgment, For I would have denied God above" (Job 31:24-28).

Trust Him Because His Strength is Great

"Who sent out the wild donkey free? And who loosed the bonds of the swift donkey, To whom I gave the wilderness for a home And the salt land for his dwelling place? He scorns the tumult of the city, The shoutings of the driver he does not hear. He explores the mountains for his pasture And searches after every green thing. Will the wild ox consent to serve you, Or will he spend the night at your manger? Can you bind the wild ox in a furrow with ropes, Or will he harrow the valleys after you? Will you trust him because his strength is great And leave your labor to him? Will you have faith in him that he will return your grain And gather it from your threshing floor" (Job 39:5-12)?

IN THE BOOK OF PSALMS

Trust in the Lord

"Tremble, and do not sin; Meditate in your heart upon your bed, and be still. Selah. Offer the sacrifices of righteousness, And trust in the Lord" (Ps. 4:4-5).

Those Who Know Your Name Will Put their Trust In You

"When my enemies turn back, They stumble and perish before You. For You have maintained my just cause; You have sat on the throne judging righteously. You have rebuked the nations, You have destroyed the wicked; You have blotted out their name forever and ever. The enemy has come to an end in perpetual ruins, And You have uprooted the cities; The very memory of them has perished. But the Lord abides forever; He has established His throne for judgment, And He will judge the world in righteousness; He will execute judgment for the peoples with equity. The Lord also will be a stronghold for the oppressed, A stronghold in times of trouble; And those who know Your name will put their trust in You, For You, O Lord, have not forsaken those who seek You" (Ps. 9:3-10).

You Made Me Trust When Upon My Mother's Breast

"Yet You are He who brought me forth from the womb; You made me trust when upon my mother's breasts. Upon You I was cast from birth; You have been my God from my mother's womb" (Ps. 22:9-10).

O My God, in You I Trust

"To You, O Lord, I lift up my soul. O my God, in You I trust, Do not let me be ashamed; Do not let my enemies exult over me. Indeed, none of those who wait for You will be ashamed; Those who deal treacherously without cause will be ashamed" (Ps. 25:1-3).

Chapter Two

I Hate Those Who Regard Vain Idols, but I Trust in the Lord

"I hate those who regard vain idols, But I trust in the Lord. I will rejoice and be glad in Your lovingkindness, Because You have seen my affliction; You have known the troubles of my soul, And You have not given me over into the hand of the enemy; You have set my feet in a large place" (Ps. 31:6-8).

But as for Me, I Trust in You, O Lord

"But as for me, I trust in You, O Lord, I say, 'You are my God.' My times are in Your hand; Deliver me from the hand of my enemies and from those who persecute me. Make Your face to shine upon Your servant; Save me in Your lovingkindness. Let me not be put to shame, O Lord, for I call upon You; Let the wicked be put to shame, let them be silent in Sheol. Let the lying lips be mute, Which speak arrogantly against the righteous With pride and contempt" (Ps. 31:14-18).

We Trust In His Holy Name

"Behold, the eye of the Lord is on those who fear Him, On those who hope for His lovingkindness, To deliver their soul from death And to keep them alive in famine. Our soul waits for the Lord; He is our help and our shield. For our heart rejoices in Him, Because we trust in His holy name. Let Your lovingkindness, O Lord, be upon us, According as we have hoped in You" (Ps. 33:18-22).

Trust In the Lord and Do Good

"Do not fret because of evildoers, Be not envious toward wrongdoers. For they will wither quickly like the grass And fade like the green herb. Trust in the Lord and do good; Dwell in the land and cultivate faithfulness. Delight yourself in the Lord; And He will give you the desires of your heart. Commit your way to the Lord, Trust also in Him, and He will do it. He will bring forth your righteousness as the light And your judgment as the noonday" (Ps. 37:1-6).

Many Will See and Fear and Trust in the Lord

"I waited patiently for the Lord; And He inclined to me and heard my cry. He brought me up out of the pit of destruction, out of the miry clay, And He set my feet upon a rock making my footsteps firm. He put a new song in my mouth, a song of praise to our God; Many will see and fear And will trust in the Lord" (Ps. 40:1-3).

Blessed is the Man Who Makes the Lord His Trust

"How blessed is the man who has made the Lord his trust, And has not turned to the proud, nor to those who lapse into falsehood. Many, O Lord my God, are the wonders which You have done, And Your thoughts toward us; There is none to compare with You. If I would declare and speak of them, They would be too numerous to count" (Ps. 40:4-5).

I Will Not Trust in My Bow

"You are my King, O God; Command victories for Jacob. Through You we will push back our adversaries; Through Your name we will trample down those who rise up against us. For I will not trust in my bow, Nor will my sword save me. But You have saved us from our adversaries, And You have put to shame those who hate us" (Ps. 44:4-7).

Even Those Who Trust in Their Wealth

"Why should I fear in days of adversity, When the iniquity of my foes surrounds me, Even those who trust in their wealth And boast in the abundance of their riches? No man can by any means redeem his brother Or give to God a ransom for him — For the redemption of his soul is costly, And he should cease trying forever — That he should live on eternally, That he should not undergo decay" (Ps. 49:5-9).

Chapter Two

I Trust in the Lovingkindness of God

"But as for me, I am like a green olive tree in the house of God; I trust in the lovingkindness of God forever and ever. I will give You thanks forever, because You have done it, And I will wait on Your name, for it is good, in the presence of Your godly ones" (Ps. 52:8-9).

I Will Trust in You

"Cast your burden upon the Lord and He will sustain you; He will never allow the righteous to be shaken. But You, O God, will bring them down to the pit of destruction; Men of bloodshed and deceit will not live out half their days. But I will trust in You" (Ps. 55:22-23).

When I am Afraid, I will Put my Trust in You

"Be gracious to me, O God, for man has trampled upon me; Fighting all day long he oppresses me. My foes have trampled upon me all day long, For they are many who fight proudly against me. When I am afraid, I will put my trust in You. In God, whose word I praise, In God I have put my trust; I shall not be afraid. What can mere man do to me? All day long they distort my words; All their thoughts are against me for evil. They attack, they lurk, They watch my steps, As they have waited to take my life. Because of wickedness, cast them forth, In anger put down the peoples, O God" (Ps. 56:1-7)!

In God I have put my Trust, I shall not be afraid

"You have taken account of my wanderings; Put my tears in Your bottle. Are they not in Your book? Then my enemies will turn back in the day when I call; This I know, that God is for me. In God, whose word I praise, In the Lord, whose word I praise, In God I have put my trust, I shall not be afraid. What can man do to me? Your vows are binding upon me, O God; I will render thank offerings to You. For You have delivered my soul from death, Indeed my feet from stumbling, So that I may walk before God In the light of the living" (Ps. 56:8-13).

Trust in Him at all Times, O People

"How long will you assail a man, That you may murder him, all of you, Like a leaning wall, like a tottering fence? They have counseled only to thrust him down from his high position; They delight in falsehood; They bless with their mouth, But inwardly they curse. Selah. My soul, wait in silence for God only, For my hope is from Him. He only is my rock and my salvation, My stronghold; I shall not be shaken. On God my salvation and my glory rest; The rock of my strength, my refuge is in God. Trust in Him at all times, O people; Pour out your heart before Him; God is a refuge for us. Selah" (Ps. 62:3-8).

Do Not Trust in Oppression

"Men of low degree are only vanity and men of rank are a lie; In the balances they go up; They are together lighter than breath. Do not trust in oppression And do not vainly hope in robbery; If riches increase, do not set your heart upon them" (Ps. 62:9-10).

The Trust of all the Ends of the Earth

"By awesome deeds You answer us in righteousness, O God of our salvation, You who are the trust of all the ends of the earth and of the farthest sea; Who establishes the mountains by His strength, Being girded with might; Who stills the roaring of the seas, The roaring of their waves, And the tumult of the peoples. They who dwell in the ends of the earth stand in awe of Your signs; You make the dawn and the sunset shout for joy" (Ps. 65:5-8).

They Did Not Trust in His Salvation

"Therefore the Lord heard and was full of wrath; And a fire was kindled against Jacob And anger also mounted against Israel, Because they did not believe in God And did not trust in His salvation. Yet He commanded the clouds above

And opened the doors of heaven; He rained down manna upon them to eat And gave them food from heaven. Man did eat the bread of angels; He sent them food in abundance. He caused the east wind to blow in the heavens And by His power He directed the south wind. When He rained meat upon them like the dust, Even winged fowl like the sand of the seas, Then He let them fall in the midst of their camp, Round about their dwellings. So they ate and were well filled, And their desire He gave to them. Before they had satisfied their desire, While their food was in their mouths, The anger of God rose against them And killed some of their stoutest ones, And subdued the choice men of Israel. In spite of all this they still sinned And did not believe in His wonderful works. So He brought their days to an end in futility And their years in sudden terror" (Ps. 78:21-33).

My Refuge and Fortress, My God Whom I Trust

"He who dwells in the shelter of the Most High Will abide in the shadow of the Almighty. I will say to the Lord, 'My refuge and my fortress, My God, in whom I trust!' For it is He who delivers you from the snare of the trapper And from the deadly pestilence. He will cover you with His pinions, And under His wings you may seek refuge; His faithfulness is a shield and bulwark" (Ps. 91:1-4).

Chapter Two

O Israel, Trust in the Lord; He is their help and their Shield

"O Israel, trust in the Lord; He is their help and their shield. O house of Aaron, trust in the Lord; He is their help and their shield. You who fear the Lord, trust in the Lord; He is their help and their shield. The Lord has been mindful of us; He will bless us; He will bless the house of Israel; He will bless the house of Aaron. He will bless those who fear the Lord, The small together with the great. May the Lord give you increase, You and your children. May you be blessed of the Lord, Maker of heaven and earth" (Ps. 115:9-15).

It is Better to Take Refuge in the Lord than to Trust in Man

"Give thanks to the Lord, for He is good; For His lovingkindness is everlasting. Oh let Israel say, 'His lovingkindness is everlasting.' Oh let the house of Aaron say, 'His lovingkindness is everlasting.' Oh let those who fear the Lord say, 'His lovingkindness is everlasting.' From my distress I called upon the Lord; The Lord answered me and set me in a large place. The Lord is for me; I will not fear; What can man do to me? The Lord is for me among those who help me; Therefore I will look with satisfaction on those who hate me. It is better to take refuge in the Lord Than to trust in man. It is better to take refuge in the Lord Than to trust in princes" (Ps. 118:1-9).

Chapter Two

I Trust in Your Word

"May Your lovingkindnesses also come to me, O Lord, Your salvation according to Your word; So I will have an answer for him who reproaches me, For I trust in Your word. And do not take the word of truth utterly out of my mouth, For I wait for Your ordinances. So I will keep Your law continually, Forever and ever. And I will walk at liberty, For I seek Your precepts. I will also speak of Your testimonies before kings And shall not be ashamed. I shall delight in Your commandments, Which I love. And I shall lift up my hands to Your commandments, Which I love; And I will meditate on Your statutes" (Ps. 119:41-48).

Those Who Trust in the Lord Are as Mount Zion

"Those who trust in the Lord Are as Mount Zion, which cannot be moved but abides forever. As the mountains surround Jerusalem, So the Lord surrounds His people From this time forth and forever. For the scepter of wickedness shall not rest upon the land of the righteous, So that the righteous will not put forth their hands to do wrong" (Ps. 125:1-3).

For I Trust in You

"Answer me quickly, O Lord, my spirit fails; Do not hide Your face from me, Or I will become like those who go down to the pit. Let me hear Your lovingkindness in the morning; For I trust in You; Teach me the way in which I should walk; For to You I lift up my soul. Deliver me, O Lord, from my enemies; I take refuge in You" (Ps. 143:7-9).

Do Not Trust in Princes, In Mortal Man

"Praise the Lord! Praise the Lord, O my soul! I will praise the Lord while I live; I will sing praises to my God while I have my being. Do not trust in princes, In mortal man, in whom there is no salvation. His spirit departs, he returns to the earth; In that very day his thoughts perish. How blessed is he whose help is the God of Jacob, Whose hope is in the Lord his God, Who made heaven and earth, The sea and all that is in them; Who keeps faith forever; Who executes justice for the oppressed; Who gives food to the hungry. The Lord sets the prisoners free" (Ps. 146:1-7).

IN THE BOOK OF PROVERBS

Trust in the Lord with All Your Heart

"My son, do not forget my teaching, But let your heart keep my commandments; For length of days and years of life And peace they will add to you. Do not let kindness and truth leave you; Bind them around your neck, Write them on the tablet of your heart. So you will find favor and good repute In the sight of God and man. Trust in the Lord with all your heart And do not lean on your own understanding. In all your ways acknowledge Him, And He will make your paths straight. Do not be wise in your own eyes; Fear the Lord and turn away from evil. It will be healing to your body And refreshment to your bones. Honor the Lord from your wealth And from the first of all your produce; So your barns will be filled with plenty And your vats will overflow with new wine. My son, do not reject the discipline of the Lord Or loathe His reproof, For whom the Lord loves He reproves, Even as a father corrects the son in whom he delights" (Pr. 3:1-12).

In Which They Trust

"A wise man scales the city of the mighty And brings down the stronghold in which they trust" (Pr. 21:22).

Your Trust May Be In the Lord

"Incline your ear and hear the words of the wise, And apply your mind to my knowledge; For it will be pleasant if you keep them within you, That they may be ready on your lips. So that your trust may be in the Lord, I have taught you today, even you. Have I not written to you excellent things Of counsels and knowledge, To make you know the certainty of the words of truth

That you may correctly answer him who sent you"
(Pr. 22:17-21)?

IN THE BOOK OF ISAIAH

I Will Trust and not Be Afraid

"Then you will say on that day, 'I will give
thanks to You, O Lord; For although You were
angry with me, Your anger is turned away, And
You comfort me. Behold, God is my salvation, I
will trust and not be afraid; For the Lord God is
my strength and song, And He has become my
salvation.' Therefore you will joyously draw water
From the springs of salvation. And in that day you
will say, 'Give thanks to the Lord, call on His
name. Make known His deeds among the peoples;
Make them remember that His name is exalted.'
Praise the Lord in song, for He has done excellent
things; Let this be known throughout the earth.
Cry aloud and shout for joy, O inhabitant of Zion,
For great in your midst is the Holy One of Israel"
(Is. 12:1-6).

Trust in the Lord Forever

"In that day this song will be sung in the
land of Judah: 'We have a strong city; He sets up
walls and ramparts for security. Open the gates,
that the righteous nation may enter, The one that
remains faithful. The steadfast of mind You will
keep in perfect peace, Because he trusts in You.

Chapter Two

Trust in the Lord forever, For in God the Lord, we have an everlasting Rock. For He has brought low those who dwell on high, the unassailable city; He lays it low, He lays it low to the ground, He casts it to the dust. The foot will trample it, The feet of the afflicted, the steps of the helpless" (Is. 26:1-6).

In Quietness and Trust is Your Strength

"The oracle concerning the beasts of the Negev. Through a land of distress and anguish, From where come lioness and lion, viper and flying serpent, They carry their riches on the backs of young donkeys And their treasures on camels' humps, To a people who cannot profit them; Even Egypt, whose help is vain and empty. Therefore, I have called her 'Rahab who has been exterminated.' Now go, write it on a tablet before them And inscribe it on a scroll, That it may serve in the time to come As a witness forever. For this is a rebellious people, false sons, Sons who refuse to listen To the instruction of the Lord; Who say to the seers, 'You must not see visions'; And to the prophets, 'You must not prophesy to us what is right, Speak to us pleasant words, Prophesy illusions. Get out of the way, turn aside from the path, Let us hear no more about the Holy One of Israel.' Therefore thus says the Holy One of Israel, 'Since you have rejected this word And have put your trust in oppression and guile, and have relied on them, Therefore this iniquity will be to you Like a breach about to fall, A bulge in a high wall,

Whose collapse comes suddenly in an instant, Whose collapse is like the smashing of a potter's jar, So ruthlessly shattered That a sherd will not be found among its pieces To take fire from a hearth Or to scoop water from a cistern.' For thus the Lord God, the Holy One of Israel, has said, 'In repentance and rest you will be saved, In quietness and trust is your strength.' But you were not willing, And you said, 'No, for we will flee on horses,' Therefore you shall flee! 'And we will ride on swift horses,' Therefore those who pursue you shall be swift. One thousand will flee at the threat of one man; You will flee at the threat of five, Until you are left as a flag on a mountain top And as a signal on a hill" (Is. 30:6-17).

Rely On Horses and Trust in Chariots

"Woe to those who go down to Egypt for help And rely on horses, And trust in chariots because they are many And in horsemen because they are very strong, But they do not look to the Holy One of Israel, nor seek the Lord! Yet He also is wise and will bring disaster And does not retract His words, But will arise against the house of evildoers And against the help of the workers of iniquity. Now the Egyptians are men and not God, And their horses are flesh and not spirit; So the Lord will stretch out His hand, And he who helps will stumble And he who is helped will fall, And all of them will come to an end together" (Is. 31:1-3).

Chapter Two

We Trust in the Lord Our God

"Then Rabshakeh said to them, 'Say now to Hezekiah, 'Thus says the great king, the king of Assyria, What is this confidence that you have? I say, 'Your counsel and strength for the war are only empty words.' Now on whom do you rely, that you have rebelled against me? Behold, you rely on the staff of this crushed reed, even on Egypt, on which if a man leans, it will go into his hand and pierce it. So is Pharaoh king of Egypt to all who rely on him. But if you say to me, 'We trust in the Lord our God,' is it not He whose high places and whose altars Hezekiah has taken away and has said to Judah and to Jerusalem, 'You shall worship before this altar'? Now therefore, come make a bargain with my master the king of Assyria, and I will give you two thousand horses, if you are able on your part to set riders on them. How then can you repulse one official of the least of my master's servants and rely on Egypt for chariots and for horsemen? Have I now come up without the Lord's approval against this land to destroy it? The Lord said to me, 'Go up against this land and destroy it'''" (Is. 36:4-10).

Let Hezekiah Make You Trust in the Lord

"Then Rabshakeh stood and cried with a loud voice in Judean and said, 'Hear the words of the great king, the king of Assyria. Thus says the king, 'Do not let Hezekiah deceive you, for he will not be able to deliver you; nor let Hezekiah make you trust in the Lord, saying, 'The Lord will surely deliver us, this city will not be given into the hand of the king of Assyria.' Do not listen to Hezekiah,' for thus says the king of Assyria, 'Make your peace with me and come out to me, and eat each of his vine and each of his fig tree and drink each of the waters of his own cistern, until I come and take you away to a land like your own land, a land of grain and new wine, a land of bread and vineyards. Beware that Hezekiah does not mislead you, saying, 'The Lord will deliver us.' Has any one of the gods of the nations delivered his land from the hand of the king of Assyria? Where are the gods of Hamath and Arpad? Where are the gods of Sepharvaim? And when have they delivered Samaria from my hand? Who among all the gods of these lands have delivered their land from my hand, that the Lord would deliver Jerusalem from my hand'" (Is. 36:13-20)?

Trust Deceive You

"Then Rabshakeh returned and found the king of Assyria fighting against Libnah, for he had heard that the king had left Lachish. When he heard them say concerning Tirhakah king of Cush, 'He has come out to fight against you,' and when he heard it he sent messengers to Hezekiah, saying, 'Thus you shall say to Hezekiah king of Judah, 'Do not let your God in whom you trust deceive you, saying, 'Jerusalem will not be given into the hand of the king of Assyria.' Behold, you have heard what the kings of Assyria have done to all the lands, destroying them completely. So will you be spared? Did the gods of those nations which my fathers have destroyed deliver them, even Gozan and Haran and Rezeph and the sons of Eden who were in Telassar? Where is the king of Hamath, the king of Arpad, the king of the city of Sepharvaim, and of Hena and Ivvah'" (Is. 37:8-13)?

They Will Be Utterly Ashamed Who Trust in Idols

"I have kept silent for a long time, I have kept still and restrained Myself. Now like a woman in labor I will groan, I will both gasp and pant. I will lay waste the mountains and hills And wither all their vegetation; I will make the rivers into coastlands And dry up the ponds. I will lead the blind by a way they do not know, In paths they do not know I will guide them. I will make darkness into light before them And rugged places into plains. These are the things I will do, And I will not leave them undone.' They will be turned back and be utterly put to shame, Who trust in idols, Who say to molten images, 'You are our gods'" (Is. 42:14-17).

Chapter Two

Let Him Trust in the Name of the Lord

"The Lord God has given Me the tongue of disciples, That I may know how to sustain the weary one with a word. He awakens Me morning by morning, He awakens My ear to listen as a disciple. The Lord God has opened My ear; And I was not disobedient Nor did I turn back. I gave My back to those who strike Me, And My cheeks to those who pluck out the beard; I did not cover My face from humiliation and spitting. For the Lord God helps Me, Therefore, I am not disgraced; Therefore, I have set My face like flint, And I know that I will not be ashamed. He who vindicates Me is near; Who will contend with Me? Let us stand up to each other; Who has a case against Me? Let him draw near to Me. Behold, the Lord God helps Me; Who is he who condemns Me? Behold, they will all wear out like a garment; The moth will eat them. Who is among you that fears the Lord, That obeys the voice of His servant, That walks in darkness and has no light? Let him trust in the name of the Lord and rely on his God. Behold, all you who kindle a fire, Who encircle yourselves with firebrands, Walk in the light of your fire And among the brands you have set ablaze. This you will have from My hand: You will lie down in torment" (Is. 50:4-11).

Chapter Two

They Trust in Confession and Speak Lies

"Behold, the Lord's hand is not so short That it cannot save; Nor is His ear so dull That it cannot hear. But your iniquities have made a separation between you and your God, And your sins have hidden His face from you so that He does not hear. For your hands are defiled with blood And your fingers with iniquity; Your lips have spoken falsehood, Your tongue mutters wickedness. No one sues righteously and no one pleads honestly. They trust in confusion and speak lies; They conceive mischief and bring forth iniquity. They hatch adders' eggs and weave the spider's web; He who eats of their eggs dies, And from that which is crushed a snake breaks forth. Their webs will not become clothing, Nor will they cover themselves with their works; Their works are works of iniquity, And an act of violence is in their hands. Their feet run to evil, And they hasten to shed innocent blood; Their thoughts are thoughts of iniquity, Devastation and destruction are in their highways. They do not know the way of peace, And there is no justice in their tracks; They have made their paths crooked, Whoever treads on them does not know peace" (Is. 59:1-8).

Chapter Two

IN THE BOOK OF JEREMAIH

The Lord Has Rejected Those in Whom You Trust

"Why do you contend with Me? You have all transgressed against Me," declares the Lord. In vain I have struck your sons; They accepted no chastening. Your sword has devoured your prophets Like a destroying lion. O generation, heed the word of the Lord. Have I been a wilderness to Israel, Or a land of thick darkness? Why do My people say, 'We are free to roam; We will no longer come to You'? Can a virgin forget her ornaments, Or a bride her attire? Yet My people have forgotten Me Days without number. How well you prepare your way To seek love! Therefore even the wicked women You have taught your ways. Also on your skirts is found The lifeblood of the innocent poor; You did not find them breaking in. But in spite of all these things, Yet you said, 'I am innocent; Surely His anger is turned away from me.' Behold, I will enter into judgment with you Because you say, 'I have not sinned.' Why do you go around so much Changing your way? Also, you will be put to shame by Egypt As you were put to shame by Assyria. From this place also you will go out With your hands on your head; For the Lord has rejected those in whom you trust, And you will not prosper with them" (Jer. 2:29-37).

Chapter Two

They Will Demolish Your Fortified Cities in Which You Trust

"Therefore, thus says the Lord, the God of hosts, 'Because you have spoken this word, Behold, I am making My words in your mouth fire And this people wood, and it will consume them. Behold, I am bringing a nation against you from afar, O house of Israel,' declares the Lord. It is an enduring nation, It is an ancient nation, A nation whose language you do not know, Nor can you understand what they say. Their quiver is like an open grave, All of them are mighty men. They will devour your harvest and your food; They will devour your sons and your daughters; They will devour your flocks and your herds; They will devour your vines and your fig trees; They will demolish with the sword your fortified cities in which you trust" (Jer. 5:14-17).

Do Not Trust in Deceptive Words

"The word that came to Jeremiah from the Lord, saying, 'Stand in the gate of the Lord's house and proclaim there this word and say, 'Hear the word of the Lord, all you of Judah, who enter by these gates to worship the Lord!'" Thus says the Lord of hosts, the God of Israel, "Amend your ways and your deeds, and I will let you dwell in this place. Do not trust in deceptive words, saying, 'This is the temple of the Lord, the temple of the Lord, the temple of the Lord.' For if you truly amend your ways and your deeds, if you truly practice justice between a man and his neighbor, if you do not oppress the alien, the orphan, or the widow, and do not shed innocent blood in this place, nor walk after other gods to your own ruin, then I will let you dwell in this place, in the land that I gave to your fathers forever and ever" (Jer. 7:1-7).

In Which You Trust

"But go now to My place which was in Shiloh, where I made My name dwell at the first, and see what I did to it because of the wickedness of My people Israel. 'And now, because you have done all these things,' declares the Lord, 'and I spoke to you, rising up early and speaking, but you did not hear, and I called you but you did not answer, therefore, I will do to the house which is called by My name, in which you trust, and to the place which I gave you and your fathers, as I did to Shiloh. I will cast you out of My sight, as I have cast out all your brothers, all the offspring of Ephraim'" (Jer. 7:12-15).

Do Not Trust Any Brother

"Oh that my head were waters And my eyes a fountain of tears, That I might weep day and night For the slain of the daughter of my people! Oh that I had in the desert A wayfarers' lodging place; That I might leave my people And go from them! For all of them are adulterers, An assembly of treacherous men. They bend their tongue like their bow; Lies and not truth prevail in the land; For they proceed from evil to evil, And they do not know Me,' declares the Lord. Let everyone be on guard against his neighbor, And do not trust any brother; Because every brother deals craftily, And every neighbor goes about as a slanderer. Everyone deceives his neighbor And does not speak the truth, They have taught their tongue to speak lies; They weary themselves committing iniquity. Your dwelling is in the midst of deceit; Through deceit they refuse to know Me,' declares the Lord" (Jer. 9:1-6).

Blessed is the Man Who Trust in the Lord

"Thus says the Lord, 'Cursed is the man who trusts in mankind And makes flesh his strength, And whose heart turns away from the Lord. For he will be like a bush in the desert And will not see when prosperity comes, But will live in stony wastes in the wilderness, A land of salt without inhabitant. Blessed is the man who trusts in the Lord And whose trust is the Lord. For he will be like a tree planted by the water, That extends its roots by a stream And will not fear when the heat comes; But its leaves will be green, And it will not be anxious in a year of drought Nor cease to yield fruit" (Jer. 17:5-8).

Chapter Two

You Have Made This People Trust in a Lie

"The word of the Lord came to Jeremiah after Hananiah the prophet had broken the yoke from off the neck of the prophet Jeremiah, saying, 'Go and speak to Hananiah, saying, 'Thus says the Lord, 'You have broken the yokes of wood, but you have made instead of them yokes of iron.' For thus says the Lord of hosts, the God of Israel, 'I have put a yoke of iron on the neck of all these nations, that they may serve Nebuchadnezzar king of Babylon; and they will serve him. And I have also given him the beasts of the field.'''" Then Jeremiah the prophet said to Hananiah the prophet, 'Listen now, Hananiah, the Lord has not sent you, and you have made this people trust in a lie. Therefore thus says the Lord, 'Behold, I am about to remove you from the face of the earth. This year you are going to die, because you have counseled rebellion against the Lord'" (Jer. 28:12-16).

He Has Made You Trust in a Lie

"Zephaniah the priest read this letter to Jeremiah the prophet. Then came the word of the Lord to Jeremiah, saying, 'Send to all the exiles, saying, 'Thus says the Lord concerning Shemaiah the Nehelamite, "Because Shemaiah has prophesied to you, although I did not send him, and he has made you trust in a lie,' therefore thus says the Lord, 'Behold, I am about to punish

Shemaiah the Nehelamite and his descendants; he will not have anyone living among this people, and he will not see the good that I am about to do to My people,' declares the Lord, 'because he has preached rebellion against the Lord"'" (Jer. 29:29-32).

Pharaoh and Those Who Trust in Him

"The Lord of hosts, the God of Israel, says, 'Behold, I am going to punish Amon of Thebes, and Pharaoh, and Egypt along with her gods and her kings, even Pharaoh and those who trust in him. I shall give them over to the power of those who are seeking their lives, even into the hand of Nebuchadnezzar king of Babylon and into the hand of his officers. Afterwards, however, it will be inhabited as in the days of old,' declares the Lord" (Jer. 46:25-26).

Because of Your Trust in Your Own Achievements

"Concerning Moab. Thus says the Lord of hosts, the God of Israel, 'Woe to Nebo, for it has been destroyed; Kiriathaim has been put to shame, it has been captured; The lofty stronghold has been put to shame and shattered. There is praise for Moab no longer; In Heshbon they have devised calamity against her: 'Come and let us cut her off from being a nation!' You too, Madmen, will be silenced; The sword will follow after you. The sound of an outcry from Horonaim, 'Devastation and great destruction!' Moab is broken, Her little ones have sounded out a cry of distress. For by the ascent of Luhith They will ascend with continual weeping; For at the descent of Horonaim They have heard the anguished cry of destruction. Flee, save your lives, That you may be like a juniper in the wilderness. For because of your trust in your own achievements and treasures, Even you yourself will be captured; And Chemosh will go off into exile Together with his priests and his princes. A destroyer will come to every city, So that no city will escape; The valley also will be ruined And the plateau will be destroyed, As the Lord has said. Give wings to Moab, For she will flee away; And her cities will become a desolation, Without inhabitants in them. Cursed be the one who does the Lord's work negligently, And cursed be the one who restrains his sword from blood" (Jer. 48:1-10).

Let Your Widows Trust in Me

"Concerning Edom. Thus says the Lord of hosts, 'Is there no longer any wisdom in Teman? Has good counsel been lost to the prudent? Has their wisdom decayed? Flee away, turn back, dwell in the depths, O inhabitants of Dedan, For I will bring the disaster of Esau upon him At the time I punish him. If grape gatherers came to you, Would they not leave gleanings? If thieves came by night, They would destroy only until they had enough. But I have stripped Esau bare, I have uncovered his hiding places So that he will not be able to conceal himself; His offspring has been destroyed along with his relatives And his neighbors, and he is no more. Leave your orphans behind, I will keep them alive; And let your widows trust in Me" (Jer. 49:7-11).

IN THE BOOK OF DANIEL

His Servants Who Put their Trust in Him

"Nebuchadnezzar responded and said, 'Blessed be the God of Shadrach, Meshach and Abed-nego, who has sent His angel and delivered His servants who put their trust in Him, violating the king's command, and yielded up their bodies so as not to serve or worship any god except their own God. Therefore I make a decree that any people, nation or tongue that speaks anything offensive against the God of Shadrach, Meshach and Abed-nego shall be torn limb from limb and their houses reduced to a rubbish heap, inasmuch as there is no other god who is able to deliver in this way.' Then the king caused Shadrach, Meshach and Abed-nego to prosper in the province of Babylon" (Da. 3:28-30).

Chapter Two

IN THE BOOK OF MICAH

Do Not Trust in a Neighbor

"Woe is me! For I am Like the fruit pickers, like the grape gatherers. There is not a cluster of grapes to eat, Or a first-ripe fig which I crave. The godly person has perished from the land, And there is no upright person among men. All of them lie in wait for bloodshed; Each of them hunts the other with a net. Concerning evil, both hands do it well. The prince asks, also the judge, for a bribe, And a great man speaks the desire of his soul; So they weave it together. The best of them is like a briar, The most upright like a thorn hedge. The day when you post your watchmen, Your punishment will come. Then their confusion will occur. Do not trust in a neighbor; Do not have confidence in a friend. From her who lies in your bosom Guard your lips. For son treats father contemptuously, Daughter rises up against her mother, Daughter-in-law against her mother-in-law; A man's enemies are the men of his own household" (Mic. 7:1-6).

IN THE BOOK OF ZEPHANIAH

She Did Not Trust in the Lord

"She heeded no voice, She accepted no instruction. She did not trust in the Lord, She did not draw near to her God" (Zep. 3:2).

Chapter Three

OBEY IN THE OLD TESTAMENT

IN THE BOOK OF GENESIS

My Son; Only Obey My Voice

"Rebekah was listening while Isaac spoke to his son Esau. So when Esau went to the field to hunt for game to bring home, Rebekah said to her son Jacob, "Behold, I heard your father speak to your brother Esau, saying, 'Bring me some game and prepare a savory dish for me, that I may eat, and bless you in the presence of the Lord before my death.' Now therefore, my son, listen to me as I command you. 'Go now to the flock and bring me two choice young goats from there, that I may prepare them as a savory dish for your father, such as he loves. Then you shall bring it to your father, that he may eat, so that he may bless you before his death.' Jacob answered his mother Rebekah, 'Behold, Esau my brother is a hairy man and I am a smooth man. Perhaps my father will feel me, then I will be as a deceiver in his sight, and I will bring upon myself a curse and not a blessing.' But his mother said to him, 'Your curse be on me, my son; only obey my voice, and go, get them for me.' So he went and got them, and brought them to his mother; and his mother made savory food such as his father loved. Then Rebekah took the best garments of Esau her elder son, which were with her in the house, and put them on Jacob her younger son. And she put the skins of the young goats on his hands and on the smooth part of his neck. She also gave the savory food and the bread, which she had made, to her son Jacob" (Ge. 27:5-17).

Obey My Voice, and Arise, Flee to Haran

"So Esau bore a grudge against Jacob because of the blessing with which his father had blessed him; and Esau said to himself, 'The days of mourning for my father are near; then I will kill my brother Jacob.' Now when the words of her elder son Esau were reported to Rebekah, she sent and called her younger son Jacob, and said to him, 'Behold your brother Esau is consoling himself concerning you by planning to kill you. Now therefore, my son, obey my voice, and arise, flee to Haran, to my brother Laban! Stay with him a few days, until your brother's fury subsides, until your brother's anger against you subsides and he forgets what you did to him. Then I will send and get you from there. Why should I be bereaved of you both in one day" (Ge. 27:41-45)?

IN THE BOOK OF EXODUS

Who Is the Lord That I Should Obey His Voice To Let Israel Go?

"And afterward Moses and Aaron came and said to Pharaoh, 'Thus says the Lord, the God of Israel, 'Let My people go that they may celebrate a feast to Me in the wilderness.'" But Pharaoh said, 'Who is the Lord that I should obey His voice to let Israel go? I do not know the Lord, and besides, I will not let Israel go.' Then they said, 'The God of the Hebrews has met with us. Please, let us go a three days' journey into the wilderness that we may sacrifice to the Lord our God, otherwise He will fall upon us with pestilence or with the sword.' But the king of Egypt said to them, 'Moses and Aaron, why do you draw the people away from their work? Get back to your labors!' Again Pharaoh said, 'Look, the people of the land are now many, and you would have them cease from their labors!' So the same day Pharaoh commanded the taskmasters over the people and their foremen, saying, 'You are no longer to give the people straw to make brick as previously; let them go and gather straw for themselves. But the quota of bricks which they were making previously, you shall impose on them; you are not to reduce any of it. Because they are lazy, therefore they cry out, 'Let us go and sacrifice to our God.' Let the labor be heavier on the men, and let them work at it so that they will pay no attention to false words" (Ex. 5:1-9).

Obey My Voice and Keep My Covenant, Then You Shall Be My Own Possession

"In the third month after the sons of Israel had gone out of the land of Egypt, on that very day they came into the wilderness of Sinai. When they set out from Rephidim, they came to the wilderness of Sinai and camped in the wilderness; and there Israel camped in front of the mountain. Moses went up to God, and the Lord called to him from the mountain, saying, 'Thus you shall say to the house of Jacob and tell the sons of Israel: 'You yourselves have seen what I did to the Egyptians, and how I bore you on eagles' wings, and brought you to Myself. Now then, if you will indeed obey My voice and keep My covenant, then you shall be My own possession among all the peoples, for all the earth is Mine; and you shall be to Me a kingdom of priests and a holy nation.' These are the words that you shall speak to the sons of Israel" (Ex. 19:1-6).

Be On Your Guard before Him and Obey His Voice; Do Not Be Rebellious Toward Him

"Behold, I am going to send an angel before you to guard you along the way and to bring you into the place which I have prepared. Be on your guard before him and obey his voice; do not be rebellious toward him, for he will not pardon your transgression, since My name is in him. But if you truly obey his voice and do all that I say, then I will be an enemy to your enemies and an adversary to your adversaries. For My angel will go before you and bring you in to the land of the Amorites, the Hittites, the Perizzites, the Canaanites, the Hivites and the Jebusites; and I will completely destroy them. You shall not worship their gods, nor serve them, nor do according to their deeds; but you shall utterly overthrow them and break their sacred pillars in pieces. But you shall serve the Lord your God, and He will bless your bread and your water; and I will remove sickness from your midst. There shall be no one miscarrying or barren in your land; I will fulfill the number of your days. I will send My terror ahead of you, and throw into confusion all the people among whom you come, and I will make all your enemies turn their backs to you. I will send hornets ahead of you so that they will drive out the Hivites, the Canaanites, and the Hittites before you. I will not drive them out before you in a single year, that the land may not become desolate and the beasts of the field become too numerous for you. I will drive them out before you little by little, until you become fruitful and take possession of the land. I will fix your boundary from the Red Sea to the sea of the Philistines, and from the wilderness to the River Euphrates; for I will deliver the inhabitants of the land into your hand, and you will drive them out before you. You shall make no covenant with them or with their gods. They shall not live in your land, because they will make you sin against Me; for if you serve their gods, it will surely be a snare to you" (Ex. 23:20-33).

Chapter Three

IN THE BOOK OF LEVITICUS

If You Do Not Obey Me, Then I Will Punish You Seven Times More For Your Sins

"But if you do not obey Me and do not carry out all these commandments, if, instead, you reject My statutes, and if your soul abhors My ordinances so as not to carry out all My commandments, and so break My covenant, I, in turn, will do this to you: I will appoint over you a sudden terror, consumption and fever that will waste away the eyes and cause the soul to pine away; also, you will sow your seed uselessly, for your enemies will eat it up. I will set My face against you so that you will be struck down before your enemies; and those who hate you will rule over you, and you will flee when no one is pursuing you. If also after these things you do not obey Me, then I will punish you seven times more for your sins. I will also break down your pride of power; I will also make your sky like iron and your earth like bronze. Your strength will be spent uselessly, for your land will not yield its produce and the trees of the land will not yield their fruit" (Le. 26:14-20).

If You Are Unwilling to Obey Me, I Will Increase the Plague on You Seven Times

"If then, you act with hostility against Me and are unwilling to obey Me, I will increase the plague on you seven times according to your sins. I will let loose among you the beasts of the field, which will bereave you of your children and destroy your cattle and reduce your number so that your roads lie deserted" (Le. 26:21-22).

If In Spite Of This You Do Not Obey

"Yet if in spite of this you do not obey Me, but act with hostility against Me, then I will act with wrathful hostility against you, and I, even I, will punish you seven times for your sins. Further, you will eat the flesh of your sons and the flesh of your daughters you will eat. I then will destroy your high places, and cut down your incense altars, and heap your remains on the remains of your idols, for My soul shall abhor you. I will lay waste your cities as well and will make your sanctuaries desolate, and I will not smell your soothing aromas. I will make the land desolate so that your enemies who settle in it will be appalled over it. You, however, I will scatter among the nations and will draw out a sword after you, as your land becomes desolate and your cities become waste" (Le. 26:27-33).

IN THE BOOK OF NUMBERS

May Obey Him

"Then Moses spoke to the Lord, saying, 'May the Lord, the God of the spirits of all flesh, appoint a man over the congregation, who will go out and come in before them, and who will lead them out and bring them in, so that the congregation of the Lord will not be like sheep which have no shepherd.' So the Lord said to Moses, "Take Joshua the son of Nun, a man in whom is the Spirit, and lay your hand on him; and have him stand before Eleazar the priest and before all the congregation, and commission him in their sight. You shall put some of your authority on him, in order that all the congregation of the sons of Israel may obey him. Moreover, he shall stand before Eleazar the priest, who shall inquire for him by the judgment of the Urim before the Lord. At his command they shall go out and at his command they shall come in, both he and the sons of Israel with him, even all the congregation.' Moses did just as the Lord commanded him; and he took Joshua and set him before Eleazar the priest and before all the congregation. Then he laid his hands on him and commissioned him, just as the Lord had spoken through Moses" (Nu. 27:15-23).

IN THE BOOK OF DEUTERONOMY

Who Will Not Obey His Father or His Mother

"If any man has a stubborn and rebellious son who will not obey his father or his mother, and when they chastise him, he will not even listen to them, then his father and mother shall seize him, and bring him out to the elders of his city at the gateway of his hometown. They shall say to the elders of his city, 'This son of ours is stubborn and rebellious, he will not obey us, he is a glutton and a drunkard.' Then all the men of his city shall stone him to death; so you shall remove the evil from your midst, and all Israel will hear of it and fear" (De. 21:18-21).

You Shall Therefore Obey the Lord Your God, and Do His Commandments and His Statutes

"Then Moses and the Levitical priests spoke to all Israel, saying, 'Be silent and listen, O Israel! This day you have become a people for the Lord your God. You shall therefore obey the Lord your God, and do His commandments and His statutes which I command you today'" (De. 27:9-10).

If You Diligently Obey the Lord Your God

"Now it shall be, if you diligently obey the Lord your God, being careful to do all His commandments which I command you today, the Lord your God will set you high above all the nations of the earth. All these blessings will come upon you and overtake you if you obey the Lord your God" (De. 28:1-2).

Chapter Three

If You Do Not Obey the Lord Your God, All These Curses Will Come Upon You

"But it shall come about, if you do not obey the Lord your God, to observe to do all His commandments and His statutes with which I charge you today, that all these curses will come upon you and overtake you" (De. 28:15).

(The rest of chapter 28 discusses all the curses.)

Because You Would Not Obey the Lord Your God

"So all these curses shall come on you and pursue you and overtake you until you are destroyed, because you would not obey the Lord your God by keeping His commandments and His statutes which He commanded you. They shall become a sign and a wonder on you and your descendants forever" (De. 28:45-46).

You Did Not Obey the Lord

"If you are not careful to observe all the words of this law which are written in this book, to fear this honored and awesome name, the Lord your God, then the Lord will bring extraordinary plagues on you and your descendants, even severe and lasting plagues, and miserable and chronic sicknesses. He will bring back on you all the diseases of Egypt of which you were afraid, and they will cling to you. Also every sickness and every plague which, not written in the book of this law, the Lord will bring on you until you are destroyed. Then you shall be left few in number, whereas you were as numerous as the stars of heaven, because you did not obey the Lord your God. It shall come about that as the Lord delighted over you to prosper you, and multiply you, so the Lord will delight over you to make you perish and destroy you; and you will be torn from the land where you are entering to possess it. Moreover, the Lord will scatter you among all peoples, from one end of the earth to the other end of the earth; and there you shall serve other gods, wood and stone, which you or your fathers have not known. Among those nations you shall find no rest, and there will be no resting place for the sole of your foot; but there the Lord will give you a trembling heart, failing of eyes, and despair of soul. So your life shall hang in doubt before you; and you will be in dread night and day, and shall have no assurance of your life. In the morning you shall say, 'Would that it were evening!' And at evening you shall say, 'Would that it were morning!' because of the dread of your heart which you dread, and for the sight of your eyes which you will see. The Lord will bring you back to Egypt in ships, by the way about which I spoke to you, 'You will never see it again!' And there you will offer yourselves for sale to your enemies as male and female slaves, but there will be no buyer" (De. 28:58-68).

Chapter Three

Return to the Lord Your God and Obey Him with All Your Heart and Soul

"So it shall be when all of these things have come upon you, the blessing and the curse which I have set before you, and you call them to mind in all nations where the Lord your God has banished you, and you return to the Lord your God and obey Him with all your heart and soul according to all that I command you today, you and your sons, then the Lord your God will restore you from captivity, and have compassion on you, and will gather you again from all the peoples where the Lord your God has scattered you. If your outcasts are at the ends of the earth, from there the Lord your God will gather you, and from there He will bring you back. The Lord your God will bring you into the land which your fathers possessed, and you shall possess it; and He will prosper you and multiply you more than your fathers" (De. 30:1-5).

You Shall Again Obey the Lord

"Moreover the Lord your God will circumcise your heart and the heart of your descendants, to love the Lord your God with all your heart and with all your soul, so that you may live. The Lord your God will inflict all these curses on your enemies and on those who hate you, who persecuted you. And you shall again obey the Lord, and observe all His commandments which I command you today. Then the Lord your God will prosper you abundantly in all the work of your hand, in the offspring of your body and in the offspring of your cattle and in the produce of your ground, for the Lord will again rejoice over you for good, just as He rejoiced over your fathers; if you obey the Lord your God to keep His commandments and His statutes which are written in this book of the law, if you turn to the Lord your God with all your heart and soul" (De. 30:6-10).

If Your Heart Turns Away and You Will Not Obey

"See, I have set before you today life and prosperity, and death and adversity; in that I command you today to love the Lord your God, to walk in His ways and to keep His commandments and His statutes and His judgments, that you may live and multiply, and that the Lord your God may bless you in the land where you are entering to possess it. But if your heart turns away and you will not obey, but are drawn away and worship other gods and serve them, I declare to you today that you shall surely perish. You will not prolong your days in the land where you are crossing the Jordan to enter and possess it. I call heaven and earth to witness against you today, that I have set before you life and death, the blessing and the curse. So choose life in order that you may live, you and your descendants, +by loving the Lord your God, by obeying His voice, and by holding fast to Him; for this is your life and the length of your days, that you may live in the land which the Lord swore to your fathers, to Abraham, Isaac, and Jacob, to give them" (De. 30:15-20).

IN THE BOOK OF JOSHUA

Just As We Obeyed Moses In All Things, So We Will Obey You

"They answered Joshua, saying, 'All that you have commanded us we will do, and wherever you send us we will go. Just as we obeyed Moses in all things, so we will obey you; only may the Lord your God be with you as He was with Moses. Anyone who rebels against your command and does not obey your words in all that you command him, shall be put to death; only be strong and courageous" (Jos. 1:16-18).

The People Said to Joshua, "We Will Serve the Lord Our God and We Will Obey His Voice."

"Then Joshua said to the people, 'You will not be able to serve the Lord, for He is a holy God. He is a jealous God; He will not forgive your transgression or your sins. If you forsake the Lord and serve foreign gods, then He will turn and do you harm and consume you after He has done good to you.' The people said to Joshua, 'No, but we will serve the Lord.' Joshua said to the people,

'You are witnesses against yourselves that you have chosen for yourselves the Lord, to serve Him.' And they said, 'We are witnesses.' 'Now therefore, put away the foreign gods which are in your midst, and incline your hearts to the Lord, the God of Israel.' The people said to Joshua, 'We will serve the Lord our God and we will obey His voice.' So Joshua made a covenant with the people that day, and made for them a statute and an ordinance in Shechem. And Joshua wrote these words in the book of the law of God; and he took a large stone and set it up there under the oak that was by the sanctuary of the Lord. Joshua said to all the people, 'Behold, this stone shall be for a witness against us, for it has heard all the words of the Lord which He spoke to us; thus it shall be for a witness against you, so that you do not deny your God.' Then Joshua dismissed the people, each to his inheritance" (Jos. 24:19-28).

IN THE BOOK OF JUDGES

They Were For Testing Israel, To Find Out If They Would Obey

"Now these are the nations which the Lord left, to test Israel by them (that is, all who had not experienced any of the wars of Canaan; only in order that the generations of the sons of Israel might be taught war, those who had not experienced it formerly). These nations are: the five lords of the Philistines and all the Canaanites and the Sidonians and the Hivites who lived in Mount Lebanon, from Mount Baal-hermon as far as Lebo-hamath. They were for testing Israel, to find out if they would obey the commandments of the Lord, which He had commanded their fathers through Moses. The sons of Israel lived among the Canaanites, the Hittites, the Amorites, the Perizzites, the Hivites, and the Jebusites; and they took their daughters for themselves as wives, and gave their own daughters to their sons, and served their gods" (Jud. 3:1-6).

IN THE BOOK OF 1 SAMUEL

Why Then Did You Not Obey the Voice of the Lord, but Rushed Upon the Spoil

"Samuel said, 'Is it not true, though you were little in your own eyes, you were made the head of the tribes of Israel? And the Lord anointed you king over Israel, and the Lord sent you on a mission, and said, 'Go and utterly destroy the sinners, the Amalekites, and fight against them until they are exterminated.' Why then did you not obey the voice of the Lord, but rushed upon the spoil and did what was evil in the sight of the Lord" (1Sa. 15:17-19)?

I Did Obey

"Then Saul said to Samuel, 'I did obey the voice of the Lord, and went on the mission on which the Lord sent me, and have brought back Agag the king of Amalek, and have utterly destroyed the Amalekites. But the people took some of the spoil, sheep and oxen, the choicest of the things devoted to destruction, to sacrifice to the Lord your God at Gilgal.' Samuel said, 'Has the Lord as much delight in burnt offerings and sacrifices As in obeying the voice of the Lord? Behold, to obey is better than sacrifice, And to heed than the fat of rams. For rebellion is as the sin of divination, and insubordination is as iniquity and idolatry. Because you have rejected the word of the Lord, He has also rejected you from being king" (1Sa. 15:20-23).

You Did Not Obey the Lord and Did Not Execute His Fierce Wrath on Amalek

"Then Samuel said to Saul, 'Why have you disturbed me by bringing me up?' And Saul answered, 'I am greatly distressed; for the Philistines are waging war against me, and God has departed from me and no longer answers me, either through prophets or by dreams; therefore I have called you, that you may make known to me what I should do.' Samuel said, 'Why then do you ask me, since the Lord has departed from you and has become your adversary? The Lord has done accordingly as He spoke through me; for the Lord has torn the kingdom out of your hand and given it to your neighbor, to David. As you did not obey the Lord and did not execute His fierce wrath on

Amalek, so the Lord has done this thing to you this day. Moreover the Lord will also give over Israel along with you into the hands of the Philistines, therefore tomorrow you and your sons will be with me. Indeed the Lord will give over the army of Israel into the hands of the Philistines'" (1Sa. 28:15-19)!

IN THE BOOK OF 2 KINGS

They Did Not Obey the Voice of the Lord Their God, but Transgressed His Covenant

"Now in the fourth year of King Hezekiah, which was the seventh year of Hoshea son of Elah king of Israel, Shalmaneser king of Assyria came up against Samaria and besieged it. At the end of three years they captured it; in the sixth year of Hezekiah, which was the ninth year of Hoshea king of Israel, Samaria was captured. Then the king of Assyria carried Israel away into exile to Assyria, and put them in Halah and on the Habor, the river of Gozan, and in the cities of the Medes, because they did not obey the voice of the Lord their God, but transgressed His covenant, even all that Moses the servant of the Lord commanded; they would neither listen nor do it" (2Ki. 18:9-12).

Chapter Three

IN THE BOOK OF ESTHER

She Did Not Obey the Command of King Ahasuerus Delivered By the Eunuchs

"'Then the king said to the wise men who understood the times — for it was the custom of the king so to speak before all who knew law and justice and were close to him: Carshena, Shethar, Admatha, Tarshish, Meres, Marsena and Memucan, the seven princes of Persia and Media who had access to the king's presence and sat in the first place in the kingdom — According to law, what is to be done with Queen Vashti, because she did not obey the command of King Ahasuerus delivered by the eunuchs?' In the presence of the king and the princes, Memucan said, 'Queen Vashti has wronged not only the king but also all the princes and all the peoples who are in all the provinces of King Ahasuerus. For the queen's conduct will become known to all the women causing them to look with contempt on their husbands by saying, 'King Ahasuerus commanded Queen Vashti to be brought in to his presence, but she did not come.' This day the ladies of Persia and Media who have heard of the queen's conduct will speak in the same way to all the king's princes, and there will be plenty of contempt and anger. If it pleases the king, let a royal edict be issued by him and let it be written in the laws of Persia and Media so that it cannot be repealed, that Vashti may no longer come into the presence of King Ahasuerus, and let the king give her royal position to another who is more worthy than she. When the king's edict which he will make is heard throughout all his kingdom, great as it is, then all women will give honor to their husbands, great and small" (Est. 1:13-20).

IN THE BOOK OF PSALMS

As Soon As They Hear, They Obey Me; Foreigners Submit To Me

"You have delivered me from the contentions of the people; You have placed me as head of the nations; A people whom I have not known serve me. As soon as they hear, they obey me; Foreigners submit to me. Foreigners fade away, And come trembling out of their fortresses" (Ps. 18:43-45).

But My People Did Not Listen To My Voice, and Israel Did Not Obey Me

"But My people did not listen to My voice, And Israel did not obey Me. So I gave them over to the stubbornness of their heart, To walk in their own devices. Oh that My people would listen to Me, That Israel would walk in My ways! I would quickly subdue their enemies And turn My hand against their adversaries. Those who hate the Lord would pretend obedience to Him, And their time of punishment would be forever. But I would feed you with the finest of the wheat, And with honey from the rock I would satisfy you" (Ps. 81:11-16).

IN THE BOOK OF ISAIAH

If You Consent and Obey, You Will Eat the Best of the Land

"'Come now, and let us reason together,' Says the Lord, 'Though your sins are as scarlet, They will be as white as snow; Though they are red like crimson, They will be like wool. If you consent and obey, You will eat the best of the land; But if you refuse and rebel, You will be devoured by the sword.' Truly, the mouth of the Lord has spoken" (Isa. 1:18-20).

Whose Law They Did Not Obey

"Who among you will give ear to this? Who will give heed and listen hereafter? Who gave Jacob up for spoil, and Israel to plunderers? Was it not the Lord, against whom we have sinned, And in whose ways they were not willing to walk, And whose law they did not obey? So He poured out on him the heat of His anger And the fierceness of battle; And it set him aflame all around, Yet he did not recognize it;And it burned him, but he paid no attention" (Isa. 42:23-25).

Chapter Three

IN THE BOOK OF JEREMIAH

Obey My Voice, and I Will Be Your God, and You Will Be My People

"Thus says the Lord of hosts, the God of Israel, 'Add your burnt offerings to your sacrifices and eat flesh. For I did not speak to your fathers, or command them in the day that I brought them out of the land of Egypt, concerning burnt offerings and sacrifices. But this is what I commanded them, saying, 'Obey My voice, and I will be your God, and you will be My people; and you will walk in all the way which I command you, that it may be well with you.' Yet they did not obey or incline their ear, but walked in their own counsels and in the stubbornness of their evil heart, and went backward and not forward. Since the day that your fathers came out of the land of Egypt until this day, I have sent you all My servants the prophets, daily rising early and sending them. Yet they did not listen to Me or incline their ear, but stiffened their neck; they did more evil than their fathers" (Jer. 7:21-26).

This Is the Nation That Did Not Obey the Voice of the Lord Their God or Accept Correction

"You shall speak all these words to them, but they will not listen to you; and you shall call to them, but they will not answer you. You shall say to them, 'This is the nation that did not obey the voice of the Lord their God or accept correction; truth has perished and has been cut off from their mouth. Cut off your hair and cast it away, And take up a lamentation on the bare heights; For the Lord has rejected and forsaken The generation of His wrath.' 'For the sons of Judah have done that which is evil in My sight,' declares the Lord, 'they have set their detestable things in the house which is called by My name, to defile it. They have built the high places of Topheth, which is in the valley of the son of Hinnom, to burn their sons and their daughters in the fire, which I did not command, and it did not come into My mind'" (Jer. 7:27-31).

Yet They Did Not Obey Or Incline Their Ear

"And the Lord said to me, 'Proclaim all these words in the cities of Judah and in the streets of Jerusalem, saying, 'Hear the words of this covenant and do them. For I solemnly warned your fathers in the day that I brought them up from the land of Egypt, even to this day, warning persistently, saying, 'Listen to My voice.' Yet they did not obey or incline their ear, but walked, each one, in the stubbornness of his evil heart; therefore I brought on them all the words of this covenant, which I commanded them to do, but they did not'" (Jer. 11:6-8).

Chapter Three

If You Will Not Obey These Words, I Swear By Myself, This House Will Become a Desolation

"Thus says the Lord, 'Go down to the house of the king of Judah, and there speak this word and say, 'Hear the word of the Lord, O king of Judah, who sits on David's throne, you and your servants and your people who enter these gates. Thus says the Lord, 'Do justice and righteousness, and deliver the one who has been robbed from the power of his oppressor. Also do not mistreat or do violence to the stranger, the orphan, or the widow; and do not shed innocent blood in this place. For if you men will indeed perform this thing, then kings will enter the gates of this house, sitting in David's place on his throne, riding in chariots and on horses, even the king himself and his servants and his people. But if you will not obey these words, I swear by Myself,' declares the Lord, 'that this house will become a desolation.'''" For thus says the Lord concerning the house of the king of Judah: 'You are like Gilead to Me, Like the summit of Lebanon; Yet most assuredly I will make you like a wilderness, Like cities which are not inhabited. For I will set apart destroyers against you, Each with his weapons; And they will cut down your choicest cedars And throw them on the fire'" (Jer. 22:1-7).

Chapter Three

Obey the Voice of the Lord Your God; and the Lord Will Change His Mind

"Then Jeremiah spoke to all the officials and to all the people, saying, 'The Lord sent me to prophesy against this house and against this city all the words that you have heard. Now therefore amend your ways and your deeds and obey the voice of the Lord your God; and the Lord will change His mind about the misfortune which He has pronounced against you. But as for me, behold, I am in your hands; do with me as is good and right in your sight. Only know for certain that if you put me to death, you will bring innocent blood on yourselves, and on this city and on its inhabitants; for truly the Lord has sent me to you to speak all these words in your hearing" (Jer. 26:12-15).

They Did Not Obey Your Voice or Walk In Your Law

"After I had given the deed of purchase to Baruch the son of Neriah, then I prayed to the Lord, saying, 'Ah Lord God! Behold, You have made the heavens and the earth by Your great power and by Your outstretched arm! Nothing is too difficult for You, who shows lovingkindness to thousands, but repays the iniquity of fathers into the bosom of their children after them, O great and mighty God. The Lord of hosts is His name; great in counsel and mighty in deed, whose eyes are open to all the ways of the sons of men, giving to everyone according to his ways and according to the fruit of his deeds; who has set signs and wonders in the land of Egypt, and even to this day both in Israel and among mankind; and You have made a name for Yourself, as at this day. You brought Your people Israel out of the land of Egypt with signs and with wonders, and with a strong hand and with an outstretched arm and with great terror; and gave them this land, which You swore to their forefathers to give them, a land flowing with milk and honey. They came in and took possession of it, but they did not obey Your voice or walk in Your law; they have done nothing of all that You commanded them to do; therefore You have made all this calamity come upon them. Behold, the siege ramps have reached the city to take it; and the city is given into the hand of the Chaldeans who fight against it, because of the sword, the famine and the pestilence; and what You have spoken has come to pass; and behold, You see it. You have said to me, O Lord God, 'Buy for yourself the field with money and call in witnesses" — although the city is given into the hand of the Chaldeans'" (Jer. 32:16-25).

Your Forefathers Did Not Obey Me or Incline Their Ear to Me

"Then the word of the Lord came to Jeremiah from the Lord, saying, 'Thus says the Lord God of Israel, 'I made a covenant with your forefathers in the day that I brought them out of the land of Egypt, from the house of bondage, saying, 'At the end of seven years each of you shall set free his Hebrew brother who has been sold to you and has served you six years, you shall send him out free from you; but your forefathers did not obey Me or incline their ear to Me. Although recently you had turned and done what is right in My sight, each man proclaiming release to his neighbor, and you had made a covenant before Me in the house which is called by My name. Yet you turned and profaned My name, and each man took back his male servant and each man his female servant whom you had set free according to their desire, and you brought them into subjection to be your male servants and female servants"' (Jer. 34:12-16).

Please Obey the Lord in What I Am Saying to You That It May Go Well With You

"Then Jeremiah said to Zedekiah, 'Thus says the Lord God of hosts, the God of Israel, 'If you will indeed go out to the officers of the king of Babylon, then you will live, this city will not be burned with fire, and you and your household will survive. But if you will not go out to the officers of the king of Babylon, then this city will be given over to the hand of the Chaldeans; and they will burn it with fire, and you yourself will not escape from their hand.'" Then King Zedekiah said to Jeremiah, 'I dread the Jews who have gone over to the Chaldeans, for they may give me over into their hand and they will abuse me.' But Jeremiah said, 'They will not give you over. Please obey the Lord in what I am saying to you, that it may go well with you and you may live. But if you keep refusing to go out, this is the word which the Lord has shown me: Then behold, all of the women who have been left in the palace of the king of Judah are going to be brought out to the officers of the king of Babylon; and those women will say, 'Your close friends Have misled and overpowered you; While your feet were sunk in the mire, They turned back'" (Jer. 38:17-22).

They Did Not Obey the Voice of the Lord

"But as soon as Jeremiah, whom the Lord their God had sent, had finished telling all the people all the words of the Lord their God — that is, all these words — Azariah the son of Hoshaiah, and Johanan the son of Kareah, and all the arrogant men said to Jeremiah, 'You are telling a lie! The Lord our God has not sent you to say, 'You are not to enter Egypt to reside there'; but Baruch the son of Neriah is inciting you against us to give us over into the hand of the Chaldeans, so they will put us to death or exile us to Babylon.' So Johanan the son of Kareah and all the commanders of the forces, and all the people, did not obey the voice of the Lord to stay in the land of Judah. But Johanan the son of Kareah and all the commanders of the forces took the entire remnant of Judah who had returned from all the nations to which they had been driven away, in order to reside in the land of Judah — the men, the women, the children, the king's daughters and every person that Nebuzaradan the captain of the bodyguard had left with Gedaliah the son of Ahikam and grandson of Shaphan, together with Jeremiah the prophet and Baruch the son of Neriah — and they entered the land of Egypt (for they did not obey the voice of the Lord) and went in as far as Tahpanhes" (Jer. 43:1-7).

IN THE BOOK OF DANIEL

All the Dominions Will Serve and Obey Him

"Thus he said: 'The fourth beast will be a fourth kingdom on the earth, which will be different from all the other kingdoms and will devour the whole earth and tread it down and crush it. As for the ten horns, out of this kingdom ten kings will arise; and another will arise after them, and he will be different from the previous ones and will subdue three kings. He will speak out against the Most High and wear down the saints of the Highest One, and he will intend to make alterations in times and in law; and they will be given into his hand for a time, times, and half a time. But the court will sit for judgment, and his dominion will be taken away, annihilated and destroyed forever. Then the sovereignty, the dominion and the greatness of all the kingdoms under the whole heaven will be given to the people of the saints of the Highest One; His kingdom will be an everlasting kingdom, and all the dominions will serve and obey Him" (Da. 7:23-27).

IN THE BOOK OF ZECHARIAH

It Will Take Place If You Completely Obey the Lord Your God

"The word of the Lord also came to me, saying, 'Take an offering from the exiles, from Heldai, Tobijah and Jedaiah; and you go the same day and enter the house of Josiah the son of Zephaniah, where they have arrived from Babylon. Take silver and gold, make an ornate crown and set it on the head of Joshua the son of Jehozadak, the high priest. Then say to him, 'Thus says the Lord of hosts, "Behold, a man whose name is Branch, for He will branch out from where He is; and He will build the temple of the Lord. Yes, it is He who will build the temple of the Lord, and He who will bear the honor and sit and rule on His throne. Thus, He will be a priest on His throne, and the counsel of peace will be between the two offices."' Now the crown will become a reminder in the temple of the Lord to Helem, Tobijah, Jedaiah and Hen the son of Zephaniah. Those who are far off will come and build the temple of the Lord.' Then you will know that the Lord of hosts has sent me to you. And it will take place if you completely obey the Lord your God" (Zec. 6:9-15).

Chapter Four

TRUST IN THE NEW TESTAMENT

IN THE BOOK OF MATTHEW

In His Name Gentiles Will Trust

"But when Jesus knew it, He withdrew from there. And great multitudes followed Him, and He healed them all. Yet He warned them not to make Him known, that it might be fulfilled which was spoken by Isaiah the prophet, saying: 'Behold! My Servant whom I have chosen, My Beloved in whom My soul is well pleased! I will put My Spirit upon Him, And He will declare justice to the Gentiles. He will not quarrel nor cry out, Nor will anyone hear His voice in the streets. A bruised reed He will not break, And smoking flax He will not quench, Till He sends forth justice to victory; And in His name Gentiles will trust"' (Mt. 12:15-21).[2]

IN THE BOOK OF MARK

How Hard It Is for Those Who trust in Riches

"Then Jesus looked around and said to His disciples, 'How hard it is for those who have riches to enter the kingdom of God!' And the disciples were astonished at His words. But Jesus answered again and said to them, 'Children, how

---

[2] From this point forward all Scripture quotations, unless otherwise noted, are from the *New King James Bible*.

hard it is for those who trust in riches to enter the kingdom of God! It is easier for a camel to go through the eye of a needle than for a rich man to enter the kingdom of God.' And they were greatly astonished, saying among themselves, 'Who then can be saved?' But Jesus looked at them and said, 'With men it is impossible, but not with God; for with God all things are possible'" (Mk. 10:23-27).

IN THE BOOK OF LUKE

Who Will Commit to your Trust the True Riches

"He who is faithful in what is least is faithful also in much; and he who is unjust in what is least is unjust also in much. Therefore if you have not been faithful in the unrighteous mammon, who will commit to your trust the true riches? And if you have not been faithful in what is another man's, who will give you what is your own? No servant can serve two masters; for either he will hate the one and love the other, or else he will be loyal to the one and despise the other. You cannot serve God and mammon" (Lk. 16:10-13).

IN THE BOOK OF JOHN

Moses, in Whom You Trust

"You search the Scriptures, for in them you think you have eternal life; and these are they which testify of Me. But you are not willing to come to Me that you may have life. I do not receive honor from men. But I know you, that you do not have the love of God in you. I have come in My Father's name, and you do not receive Me; if another comes in his own name, him you will receive. How can you believe, who receive honor from one another, and do not seek the honor that comes from the only God? Do not think that I shall accuse you to the Father; there is one who accuses you — Moses, in whom you trust. For if you believed Moses, you would believe Me; for he wrote about Me. But if you do not believe his writings, how will you believe My words" (Jn. 5:39-47)?

IN THE BOOK OF 2 CORINTHIANS

We Shall Not Trust in Ourselves

"For we do not want you to be ignorant, brethren, of our trouble which came to us in Asia: that we were burdened beyond measure, above strength, so that we despaired even of life. Yes, we had the sentence of death in ourselves, that we should not trust in ourselves but in God who raises the dead, who delivered us from so great a death, and does deliver us; in whom we trust that He will still deliver us, you also helping together in prayer for us, that thanks may be given by many persons on our behalf for the gift granted to us through many" (2Co. 1:8-11).

Chapter Four

I Trust You Will Understand

"For our boasting is this: the testimony of our conscience that we conducted ourselves in the world in simplicity and godly sincerity, not with fleshly wisdom but by the grace of God, and more abundantly toward you. For we are not writing any other things to you than what you read or understand. Now I trust you will understand, even to the end (as also you have understood us in part), that we are your boast as you also are ours, in the day of the Lord Jesus" (2Co. 1:12-14).

We Have Such Trust through Christ Toward God

"And we have such trust through Christ toward God. Not that we are sufficient of ourselves to think of anything as being from ourselves, but our sufficiency is from God, who also made us sufficient as ministers of the new covenant, not of the letter but of the Spirit; for the letter kills, but the Spirit gives life" (2Co. 3:4-6).

I Also Trust are Well Known in Your consciences

"Knowing, therefore, the terror of the Lord, we persuade men; but we are well known to God, and I also trust are well known in your consciences. For we do not commend ourselves again to you, but give you opportunity to boast on our behalf, that you may have an answer for those who boast in appearance and not in heart. For if we are beside ourselves, it is for God; or if we are of sound mind, it is for you. For the love of Christ compels us, because we judge thus: that if One died for all, then all died; and He died for all, that those who live should live no longer for themselves, but for Him who died for them and rose again" (2Co. 5:11-15).

I Trust That You Will Know

"Examine yourselves as to whether you are in the faith. Test yourselves. Do you not know yourselves, that Jesus Christ is in you? — unless indeed you are disqualified. But I trust that you will know that we are not disqualified. Now I pray to God that you do no evil, not that we should appear approved, but that you should do what is honorable, though we may seem disqualified. For we can do nothing against the truth, but for the truth. For we are glad when we are weak and you are strong. And this also we pray, that you may be made complete. Therefore I write these things being absent, lest being present I should use sharpness, according to the authority which the Lord has given me for edification and not for destruction" (2Co. 13:5-10).

Chapter Four

IN THE BOOK OF PHILIPPIANS

But I Trust in the Lord Jesus to Send Timothy

"But I trust in the Lord Jesus to send Timothy to you shortly, that I also may be encouraged when I know your state. For I have no one like-minded, who will sincerely care for your state. For all seek their own, not the things which are of Christ Jesus. But you know his proven character, that as a son with his father he served with me in the gospel. Therefore I hope to send him at once, as soon as I see how it goes with me. But I trust in the Lord that I myself shall also come shortly. Yet I considered it necessary to send to you Epaphroditus, my brother, fellow worker, and fellow soldier, but your messenger and the one who ministered to my need; since he was longing for you all, and was distressed because you had heard that he was sick. For indeed he was sick almost unto death; but God had mercy on him, and not only on him but on me also, lest I should have sorrow upon sorrow. Therefore I sent him the more eagerly, that when you see him again you may rejoice, and I may be less sorrowful. Receive him therefore in the Lord with all gladness, and hold such men in esteem; because for the work of Christ he came close to death, not regarding his life, to supply what was lacking in your service toward me" (Php. 2:19-30).

Chapter Four

IN THE BOOK OF 1 TIMOTHY

Which Was Committed To My Trust

"But we know that the law is good if one uses it lawfully, knowing this: that the law is not made for a righteous person, but for the lawless and insubordinate, for the ungodly and for sinners, for the unholy and profane, for murderers of fathers and murderers of mothers, for manslayers, for fornicators, for sodomites, for kidnappers, for liars, for perjurers, and if there is any other thing that is contrary to sound doctrine, according to the glorious gospel of the blessed God which was committed to my trust" (1Ti. 1:8-11).

Because We Trust in the Living God

"If you instruct the brethren in these things, you will be a good minister of Jesus Christ, nourished in the words of faith and of the good doctrine which you have carefully followed. But reject profane and old wives' fables, and exercise yourself toward godliness. For bodily exercise profits a little, but godliness is profitable for all things, having promise of the life that now is and of that which is to come. This is a faithful saying and worthy of all acceptance. For to this end we both labor and suffer reproach, because we trust in the living God, who is the Savior of all men, especially of those who believe" (1Ti. 4:6-10).

Chapter Four

Nor To Trust in Uncertain Riches

"Command those who are rich in this present age not to be haughty, nor to trust in uncertain riches but in the living God, who gives us richly all things to enjoy. Let them do good, that they be rich in good works, ready to give, willing to share, storing up for themselves a good foundation for the time to come, that they may lay hold on eternal life" (1Ti. 6:17-19).

What Was Committed To Your Trust

"O Timothy! Guard what was committed to your trust, avoiding the profane and idle babblings and contradictions of what is falsely called knowledge — by professing it some have strayed concerning the faith. Grace be with you. Amen" (1Ti. 6:20-21).

IN THE BOOK OF PHILEMON

I Trust Your Prayers

"But, meanwhile, also prepare a guest room for me, for I trust that through your prayers I shall be granted to you" (Phm. 1:22).

Chapter Four

IN THE BOOK OF HEBREWS

I Will Put My Trust in Him

"For it was fitting for Him, for whom are all things and by whom are all things, in bringing many sons to glory, to make the captain of their salvation perfect through sufferings. For both He who sanctifies and those who are being sanctified are all of one, for which reason He is not ashamed to call them brethren, saying: 'I will declare Your name to My brethren; In the midst of the assembly I will sing praise to You.' And again: 'I will put My trust in Him.' And again: 'Here am I and the children whom God has given Me'" (Heb. 2:10-13).

Chapter Five

OBEY IN THE NEW TESTAMENT

IN THE BOOK OF MATTHEW

What Kind of a Man Is This, That Even the Winds and the Sea Obey Him?

"Now when Jesus saw a crowd around Him, He gave orders to depart to the other side of the sea. Then a scribe came and said to Him, 'Teacher, I will follow You wherever You go.' Jesus said to him, 'The foxes have holes and the birds of the air have nests, but the Son of Man has nowhere to lay His head.' Another of the disciples said to Him, 'Lord, permit me first to go and bury my father.' But Jesus said to him, 'Follow Me, and allow the dead to bury their own dead.' When He got into the boat, His disciples followed Him. And behold, there arose a great storm on the sea, so that the boat was being covered with the waves; but Jesus Himself was asleep. And they came to Him and woke Him, saying, 'Save us, Lord; we are perishing!' He said to them, 'Why are you afraid, you men of little faith?' Then He got up and rebuked the winds and the sea, and it became perfectly calm. The men were amazed, and said, 'What kind of a man is this, that even the winds and the sea obey Him'" (Mt. 8:18-27)?[3]

---

[3] From this point forward all Scripture quotations, unless otherwise noted, are from the *New American Standard Bible.*

Chapter Five

IN THE BOOK OF MARK

He Commands Even the Unclean Spirits, and They Obey Him

"They went into Capernaum; and immediately on the Sabbath He entered the synagogue and began to teach. They were amazed at His teaching; for He was teaching them as one having authority, and not as the scribes. Just then there was a man in their synagogue with an unclean spirit; and he cried out, saying, 'What business do we have with each other, Jesus of Nazareth? Have You come to destroy us? I know who You are — the Holy One of God!' And Jesus rebuked him, saying, 'Be quiet, and come out of him!' Throwing him into convulsions, the unclean spirit cried out with a loud voice and came out of him. They were all amazed, so that they debated among themselves, saying, 'What is this? A new teaching with authority! He commands even the unclean spirits, and they obey Him.' Immediately the news about Him spread everywhere into all the surrounding district of Galilee" (Mk. 1:21-28).

Who Then Is This, That Even the Wind and the Sea Obey Him?

"On that day, when evening came, He said to them, 'Let us go over to the other side.' Leaving the crowd, they took Him along with them in the boat, just as He was; and other boats were with

Him. And there arose a fierce gale of wind, and the waves were breaking over the boat so much that the boat was already filling up. Jesus Himself was in the stern, asleep on the cushion; and they woke Him and said to Him, 'Teacher, do You not care that we are perishing?' And He got up and rebuked the wind and said to the sea, 'Hush, be still.' And the wind died down and it became perfectly calm. And He said to them, 'Why are you afraid? Do you still have no faith?' They became very much afraid and said to one another, 'Who then is this, that even the wind and the sea obey Him'" (Mk. 4:35-41)?

IN THE BOOK OF LUKE

They Obey Him

"Now on one of those days Jesus and His disciples got into a boat, and He said to them, 'Let us go over to the other side of the lake.' So they launched out. But as they were sailing along He fell asleep; and a fierce gale of wind descended on the lake, and they began to be swamped and to be in danger. They came to Jesus and woke Him up, saying, 'Master, Master, we are perishing!' And He got up and rebuked the wind and the surging waves, and they stopped, and it became calm. And He said to them, 'Where is your faith?' They were fearful and amazed, saying to one another, 'Who then is this, that He commands even the winds and the water, and they obey Him'" (Lk. 8:22-25)?

Say To This Mulberry Tree, "Be Uprooted and Be Planted In the Sea"; and It Would Obey You.

"The apostles said to the Lord, 'Increase our faith!' And the Lord said, 'If you had faith like a mustard seed, you would say to this mulberry tree, 'Be uprooted and be planted in the sea'; and it would obey you'" (Lk. 17:5-6).

IN THE BOOK OF JOHN

He Who Does Not Obey the Son Will Not See Life, But the Wrath of God Abides On Him

"He who comes from above is above all, he who is of the earth is from the earth and speaks of the earth. He who comes from heaven is above all. What He has seen and heard, of that He testifies; and no one receives His testimony. He who has received His testimony has set his seal to this, that God is true. For He whom God has sent speaks the words of God; for He gives the Spirit without measure. The Father loves the Son and has given all things into His hand. He who believes in the Son has eternal life; but he who does not obey the Son will not see life, but the wrath of God abides on him" (Jn. 3:31-36).

Chapter Five

IN THE BOOK OF ACTS

We Must Obey God Rather Than Men

"When they had brought them, they stood them before the Council. The high priest questioned them, saying, 'We gave you strict orders not to continue teaching in this name, and yet, you have filled Jerusalem with your teaching and intend to bring this man's blood upon us.' But Peter and the apostles answered, 'We must obey God rather than men. The God of our fathers raised up Jesus, whom you had put to death by hanging Him on a cross. He is the one whom God exalted to His right hand as a Prince and a Savior, to grant repentance to Israel, and forgiveness of sins. And we are witnesses of these things; and so is the Holy Spirit, whom God has given to those who obey Him" (Ac. 5:27-32).

IN THE BOOK OF ROMANS

Do Not Obey the Truth, but Obey Unrighteousness, Wrath and Indignation

"Therefore you have no excuse, everyone of you who passes judgment, for in that which you judge another, you condemn yourself; for you who judge practice the same things. And we know that the judgment of God rightly falls upon those who practice such things. But do you suppose this, O man, when you pass judgment on those who practice such things and do the same yourself, that you will escape the judgment of God? Or do you think lightly of the riches of His kindness and tolerance and patience, not knowing that the kindness of God leads you to repentance? But because of your stubbornness and unrepentant heart you are storing up wrath for yourself in the day of wrath and revelation of the righteous judgment of God, who WILL RENDER TO EACH PERSON ACCORDING TO HIS DEEDS: to those who by perseverance in doing good seek for glory and honor and immortality, eternal life; but to those who are selfishly ambitious and do not obey the truth, but obey unrighteousness, wrath and indignation. There will be tribulation and distress for every soul of man who does evil, of the Jew first and also of the Greek, but glory and honor and peace to everyone who does good, to the Jew first and also to the Greek. For there is no partiality with God" (Ro. 2:1-11).

Do Not Let Sin Reign in Your Mortal Body So That You Obey Its Lusts

"Therefore do not let sin reign in your mortal body so that you obey its lusts, and do not go on presenting the members of your body to sin as instruments of unrighteousness; but present yourselves to God as those alive from the dead, and your members as instruments of righteousness to God. For sin shall not be master over you, for you are not under law but under grace" (Ro. 6:12-14).

You Are Slaves of the One Whom You Obey

"What then? Shall we sin because we are not under law but under grace? May it never be! Do you not know that when you present yourselves to someone as slaves for obedience, you are slaves of the one whom you obey, either of sin resulting in death, or of obedience resulting in righteousness? But thanks be to God that though you were slaves of sin, you became obedient from the heart to that form of teaching to which you were committed, and having been freed from sin, you became slaves of righteousness. I am speaking in human terms because of the weakness of your flesh. For just as you presented your members as slaves to impurity and to lawlessness, resulting in further lawlessness, so now present your members as slaves to righteousness, resulting in sanctification" (Ro. 6:15-19).

IN THE BOOK OF EPHESIANS

Children, Obey Your Parents in the Lord, For This Is Right

"Children, obey your parents in the Lord, for this is right. HONOR YOUR FATHER AND MOTHER (which is the first commandment with a promise), SO THAT IT MAY BE WELL WITH

YOU, AND THAT YOU MAY LIVE LONG ON THE EARTH" (Eph. 6:1-3).

IN THE BOOK OF COLOSSIANS

Slaves, In All Things Obey Those Who Are Your Masters on Earth

"Slaves, in all things obey those who are your masters on earth, not with external service, as those who merely please men, but with sincerity of heart, fearing the Lord. Whatever you do, do your work heartily, as for the Lord rather than for men, knowing that from the Lord you will receive the reward of the inheritance. It is the Lord Christ whom you serve. For he who does wrong will receive the consequences of the wrong which he has done, and that without partiality" (Col. 3:22-25).

IN THE BOOK OF 2 THESSALONIANS

To Those Who Do Not Obey the Gospel Of Our Lord Jesus

"We ought always to give thanks to God for you, brethren, as is only fitting, because your faith is greatly enlarged, and the love of each one of you toward one another grows ever greater; therefore, we ourselves speak proudly of you among the churches of God for your perseverance and faith in the midst of all your persecutions and afflictions which you endure. This is a plain indication of God's righteous judgment so that you will be considered worthy of the kingdom of God, for which indeed you are suffering. For after all it is only just for God to repay with affliction those who afflict you, and to give relief to you who are afflicted and to us as well when the Lord Jesus will be revealed from heaven with His mighty angels in flaming fire, dealing out retribution to those who do not know God and to those who do not obey the gospel of our Lord Jesus. These will pay the penalty of eternal destruction, away from the presence of the Lord and from the glory of His power, when He comes to be glorified in His saints on that day, and to be marveled at among all who have believed — for our testimony to you was believed. To this end also we pray for you always, that our God will count you worthy of your calling, and fulfill every desire for goodness and the work of faith with power, so that the name of our Lord Jesus will be glorified in you, and you in Him, according to the grace of our God and the Lord Jesus Christ" (2Th. 1:3-12).

Obey Our Instruction

"If anyone does not obey our instruction in this letter, take special note of that person and do not associate with him, so that he will be put to shame. Yet do not regard him as an enemy, but admonish him as a brother" (2Th. 3:14-15).

Chapter Five

IN THE BOOK OF HEBREWS

He Became To All Those Who Obey Him the Source of Eternal Salvation

"So also Christ did not glorify Himself so as to become a high priest, but He who said to Him, "YOU ARE MY SON, TODAY I HAVE BEGOTTEN YOU"; just as He says also in another passage, "YOU ARE A PRIEST FOREVER ACCORDING TO THE ORDER OF MELCHIZEDEK." In the days of His flesh, He offered up both prayers and supplications with loud crying and tears to the One able to save Him from death, and He was heard because of His piety. Although He was a Son, He learned obedience from the things which He suffered. And having been made perfect, He became to all those who obey Him the source of eternal salvation, being designated by God as a high priest according to the order of Melchizedek" (Heb. 5:5-10).

Obey Your Leaders and Submit To Them

"Obey your leaders and submit to them, for they keep watch over your souls as those who will give an account. Let them do this with joy and not with grief, for this would be unprofitable for you" (Heb. 13:17).

Chapter Five

IN THE BOOK OF JAMES

We Put the Bits into the Horses' Mouths So That They Will Obey Us

"Let not many of you become teachers, my brethren, knowing that as such we will incur a stricter judgment. For we all stumble in many ways. If anyone does not stumble in what he says, he is a perfect man, able to bridle the whole body as well. Now if we put the bits into the horses' mouths so that they will obey us, we direct their entire body as well. Look at the ships also, though they are so great and are driven by strong winds, are still directed by a very small rudder wherever the inclination of the pilot desires. So also the tongue is a small part of the body, and yet it boasts of great things. See how great a forest is set aflame by such a small fire! And the tongue is a fire, the very world of iniquity; the tongue is set among our members as that which defiles the entire body, and sets on fire the course of our life, and is set on fire by hell. For every species of beasts and birds, of reptiles and creatures of the sea, is tamed and has been tamed by the human race. But no one can tame the tongue; it is a restless evil and full of deadly poison. With it we bless our Lord and Father, and with it we curse men, who have been made in the likeness of God; from the same mouth come both blessing and cursing. My brethren, these things ought not to be this way. Does a fountain send out from the same opening both fresh and bitter water? Can a fig tree, my brethren, produce olives, or a vine produce figs? Nor can salt water produce fresh" (Jas. 3:1-12).

IN THE BOOK OF 1 PETER

To Obey Jesus Christ and Be Sprinkled With His Blood

"Peter, an apostle of Jesus Christ, To those who reside as aliens, scattered throughout Pontus, Galatia, Cappadocia, Asia, and Bithynia, who are chosen according to the foreknowledge of God the Father, by the sanctifying work of the Spirit, to obey Jesus Christ and be sprinkled with His blood: May grace and peace be yours in the fullest measure" (1Pe. 1:1-2).

What Will Be the Outcome For Those Who Do Not Obey the Gospel of God?

"Beloved, do not be surprised at the fiery ordeal among you, which comes upon you for your testing, as though some strange thing were happening to you; but to the degree that you share the sufferings of Christ, keep on rejoicing, so that also at the revelation of His glory you may rejoice with exultation. If you are reviled for the name of Christ, you are blessed, because the Spirit of glory and of God rests on you. Make sure that none of you suffers as a murderer, or thief, or evildoer, or a troublesome meddler; but if anyone suffers as a

Christian, he is not to be ashamed, but is to glorify God in this name. For it is time for judgment to begin with the household of God; and if it begins with us first, what will be the outcome for those who do not obey the gospel of God? AND IF IT IS WITH DIFFICULTY THAT THE RIGHTEOUS IS SAVED, WHAT WILL BECOME OF THE GODLESS MAN AND THE SINNER? Therefore, those also who suffer according to the will of God shall entrust their souls to a faithful Creator in doing what is right" (1Pe. 4:12-19).

DAILY FAITH CONFESSIONS

(These are not direct quotations from the Bible but are paraphrased confessions based on scripture.)
SAY THEM OUT LOUD.

I am God's child (Jn. 1:12). I am royalty (1 Pet. 2:9). I am hidden with Christ in God (Col. 3:3). I am united with the Lord (1 Cor. 6:17). I am a friend of Christ (Jn. 15:15). I am raised up with Him, and seated with Him in heavenly places in Christ Jesus (Eph. 2:6). I was bought with a price (1 Cor. 6:19-20). I am blessed when I come in, and blessed shall I be when I go out (Deut. 28:6). I am a personal witness of Christ (Acts 1:8). I am a saint who prays in the Holy Spirit to keep myself in the love of God (Jude 1:20-21). I draw near with confidence to the throne of grace (Heb. 4:16). I have been adopted by the Father (Eph. 1:5). I am the salt and light of the earth (Mt. 5:13). I am the head and not the tail, and I am above, and not underneath (Deut. 28:13). I have authority to trample serpents and scorpions and over all the power of the enemy (Lk. 10:19). I am a member of the body of Christ (1 Cor. 12:27). God blessed me to be fruitful, and multiply, and replenish the earth, and subdue it: and have dominion (Gen. 1:28). I cannot be separated from God's love (Ro. 8:39). The good work God has begun in me will be perfected (Phil. 1:5). I can do all things through Christ who strengthens me (Phil. 4:13). No weapon that is formed against me will prosper (Is. 54:17). So then faith cometh by hearing, and hearing by the word of God (Ro. 10:17 KJV). Faith is my currency to operate in the kingdom of God (Ro. 14:23). I am God's workmanship created in Christ Jesus for good works, which God prepared beforehand (Eph. 2:10). I have been appointed to bear fruit, and that my fruit would remain (Jn. 15:16). I am being wise when I am winning souls for King Jesus (Pr. 11:30). My body is the temple of the Holy Spirit (1 Cor. 6:19). I have access to God through the Holy Spirit (Eph. 2:18). I have been justified (Ro. 5:1). Therefore there is now no condemnation for those who are in Christ Jesus (Ro. 8:1). Greater is He who is in me than he who is in the world (1 Jn. 4:4). I will do greater works than Jesus because He went to the Father (Jn. 14:12). As God was with Moses, He will be with me; God will not fail me or forsake me (Jos. 1:5). I see myself the way God see me. God sees me as a king (Gen, 17:6, Rev. 1:6) God sees me as royalty (1 Pet. 2:9). God sees me as the righteousness of God in Christ, bold as a lion (Ro. 3:22, Pr. 28:1). God sees me without spot or wrinkle because of the blood of Jesus (1 Pet. 1:19). I am having faith for big things because God owns everything and I'm His son (Ps. 24:1). No man will be able to stand before me all the days of my life (Jos. 1:5). My Father is glorified by this that I bear much fruit, and proves I'm a disciple (see Jn. 15:8). I think big and confess big things because God is big (Ps. 24:1). I will respect God for the big God that He is and my mouth will create whatever I want (Lk. 6:45). I no longer think of millions, my renewed mind thinks of billions because the wealth of the wicked is laid up for the righteous (Pr. 13:22). The sinner's job is to gather and collect for the one who is good in God's sight (Ecc. 2:26). Redemption is not complete without prosperity. Jesus hung on the cross so I can have the whole package, not just salvation (2 Cor. 8:9). I don't have to qualify, Jesus has qualified me. Jesus reversed the curse. The devil is a liar, and Jesus is the Messiah. Jesus is made unto me wisdom, righteousness, sanctification, and redemption (1 Cor. 1:30). I submit to God, I resist the devil and he flees from me (Jas. 4:7). For God has not given me the spirit of fear; but of power, and of love, and of a sound mind (2 Tim. 1:7). The Holy Spirit will teach me all things (Jn. 14:26). The Holy Spirit will guide me into all truth (Jn.16:13). The Holy Spirit abides in me, and I don't need anyone to teach me, but the anointing teaches me all things (1 Jn. 2:27). I quench fiery darts from the wicked one with the shield of faith (Eph. 6:16). I stand firm against the schemes of the devil (Eph. 6:11). I already have the victory and Satan cannot back me up. I advance and hold. Advance and hold to victory after victory (2 Cor. 2:14). I walk in love and live by faith (Gal. 5:6). I have been redeemed from the curse of the law, poverty, sickness, and spiritual death (Gal. 3:13; Deut. 28). I bear much fruit. I'm God's workmanship created beforehand for good works (Eph. 2:10). God's favor is on my life (Ps. 3:8). God blesses me and His favor surrounds me as with a shield (Ps. 5:12). The kingdom of God is within me (Lk. 17:21). I have a production plant inside of me that bears fruit to change the world (Gen. 1:28). God gives me power to get wealth to establish His covenant on earth (Deut. 8:18). I am blessed to be a blessing (Gen. 12:2). I have Satan on the run and will make a mockery of him (Jas. 4:7). No man will be able to stand before me all the days of my life (Jos. 1:5). Faith works through love and love never fails (Gal. 5:6; 1 Cor. 13:8). I will spend eternity with Jesus.

PRAYER FOR SALVATION

Say the following prayer out loud.

Heavenly Father, I am a sinner and I need a Savior. I confess Jesus Christ as the Lord of my life. I repent of all my sins. Father, I truly believe you raised Jesus from the dead. I pray this prayer in Jesus' name. Father, I am your child because Jesus is my Lord. I want to receive the fullness of the Holy Spirit. Holy Spirit come into me and fill me so I can be a mighty witness for King Jesus. I pray this prayer in Jesus' name. Amen.

PRAYER FOR BAPTISM OF THE HOLY SPIRIT

Say the following prayer out loud.

Father, I am your child because Jesus is my Lord. Jesus said, "How much more shall your heavenly Father give the Holy Spirit to those who ask Him." I ask you now in the name of Jesus to fill me with the Holy Spirit. Thank you, Father, I received the baptism of the Holy Spirit by faith. I yield my vocal organs and expect to speak in tongues as the Holy Spirit gives me utterance in Jesus name. Father, I plan to pray in the Holy Spirit building myself up on my most holy faith, and keep myself in the love of God, as mentioned in Jude 20 and 21. In Jesus name I decree it. Amen.

ABOUT THE AUTHOR

Eugene Carvalho is an administrator, a Christian author of seventy-seven books, and the founder of Receiving by Faith. God uses him in the offices of pastor, evangelist and prophet. He holds a bachelor's degree in biblical studies and a double minor in pastoral ministry and world missions. He also holds a master's degree in practical theology. Eugene prayed for a translator and God sent his wife Mercedes who has a six-year degree in Spanish from a university in Tampico, Mexico. They have participated in evangelism in the streets of Mexico for many years. They have also traveled to churches all over the United States and the nation of Mexico winning souls and preaching the gospel of the kingdom. Their website for their ministry is: www.receivingbyfaith.org.

BOOKS BY EUGENE IN ENGLISH

For a complete list of other books by Eugene visit receivingbyfaith.org or amazon.com.

Receiving by Faith
Faith for Every Day: 365 Daily Devotions
Faith Cometh by Hearing, and Hearing by the
Word of God
Faith, Hope, and Love
Walk in Love and Live by Faith
Topical Christian Handbook and Scripture Guide
The Gospel Is the Power of God unto Salvation
Seed Time and Harvest Time
Your New Identity in Christ
The Cross and the Blood
The Holy Spirit
The Attributes of God
The Favor of God
The Glory of God
The Grace of God
The Power of God
The Promises of God
The Spirit of God
The Throne of God
The New Testament Church: A Survey from the
Book of Ephesians
Vengeance and Recompense
God's Angel's
Prayer and Fasting
God's Mighty Prophets
A Survey of Jesus Through the Epistles

Old Testament Miracles
New Testament Miracles
The Psalms of David
The Names of Jesus
Mountain Moving Confessions
Visions and Dreams
Blessed Beyond Measure
The Righteous Will Flourish like The Palm Tree
Christ Heals: What the Bible Has to Say
My Peace I Give to You
Balancing Grace and Truth
Praise and Worship Changes Everything
Understanding the Importance of Authority
If You Are Willing and Obedient
Have Life More Abundantly
Sing Unto the Lord a New Song
The Power of the Tongue
The Supernatural: What the Bible Has to Say
The Truth Will Make You Free
Joy in the Holy Ghost
Praise Is Powerful: What the Bible Has to Say
Stewardship Regarding Our Finances
Love, Joy, and Peace Are Fruit of the Holy Ghost
Oh, Give Thanks to the Lord for He Is Good
The Kingdom of Heaven is at Hand
Acquiring Wisdom Is Vital
Grace and Mercy: What the Bible Has to Say
God Is Faithful: What the Bible Has to Say
God Is Love: What the Bible Has to Say
The God of Hope: What the Bible Has to Say
Pearls of Wisdom and Gems of Knowledge
Regarding Christianity

Victory is Mine, Joy is Mine, Peace Is Mine: I Told
Satan to Get Thee Behind
The Master's Gems
Striving Toward Perfection
For the Kingdom of God Is Righteousness, Peace
and Joy in the Holy Ghost
Encountering Proverbs, Ecclesiastes, and Song of
Solomon Through a Topical Survey
God's Feasts and Festivals
Speaking the Truth in Love
Spiritual Formation: Unleashing the Kingdom of
God within You
Prayer and Praise: The Big Artillery
Apostles and Prophets: The Foundation of the
Church
Be Strong and Courageous
Covenant: A Concise Survey
Sow Then Reap a Harvest
Grace and Peace Be Multiplied Unto You
Your Word Is a Lamp to Me Feet
Prayer Is Powerful: What the Bible Has to Say
My People Are Destroyed By Lack of Knowledge
God Deserves Pure Worship
The Lord Requires Integrity: The Major Element of
Leadership
A Topical Look at the Book of Deuteronomy
A Topical Look at the Book of Psalms
A Topical Look at the Book of Proverbs
A Topical Look at the Book of Isaiah
A Topical Look at the Book of John
A Topical Look at the Book of Hebrews
A Topical Look at the Book of Revelation

BOOKS BY EUGENE IN SPANISH

Los Salmos de David
Las Promesas de Dios
Lo Sobrenatural: Lo que la Bíblia Tiene que Decir
Una Mirada Topica Del Libro De Los Salmos
Dios es Amor: Lo que la Biblia Tiene que Decir
La Adquisición de la Sabiduría es Vital: Lo que la
Biblia Tiene que Decir

NOTES

NOTES

<u>NOTES</u>

www.ingramcontent.com/pod-product-compliance
Lightning Source LLC
Chambersburg PA
CBHW072202280526
45788CB00002B/848

* 9 7 8 1 5 4 2 4 0 9 2 8 5 *